THE LAWS OF
EVERY-DAY LIFE

THOR WRESTLING WITH ELLI

THE LAWS OF
EVERY-DAY LIFE

by

H. O. Arnold-Forster

YESTERDAY'S CLASSICS

ITHACA, NEW YORK

ISBN: 978-1-63334-066-4

Yesterday's Classics, LLC

PO Box 339

Ithaca, NY 14851

PREFACE

THIS volume is laid before the public in the hope that it may afford some slight help to those who are compelled to form and give effect to their opinion on matters concerning the welfare of our country. It has been too much the fashion to assume that the great rules by which the acts of a wise government ought to be dictated, are matters with which specialists, whether they be politicians or officials, are alone required to make themselves familiar. Now that the actual government of the country is in the hands of many millions, whatever justification there may originally have been for this supposition has passed away; and it has become absolutely necessary that those who have *power* should add to it *knowledge.* This book is not in any way intended to be a manual in the art of government, or of political economy; it is simply intended to show that there are certain great laws and rules underlying our national life which it is our interest to learn and which it is to our advantage to obey. In the following pages a few examples of these laws and rules are given, not with the object of teaching people the whole of the facts connected with them, but to give some sort of notion of the *kind of problems* which may present themselves to every British citizen, and to convey an idea of the way in which the correct or incorrect solution of these problems may affect the daily lives of all of us.

In an elementary work, especially in a work which is intended to be suggestive rather than exhaustive, very great omissions are inevitable. This is especially the case in those chapters of the present volume which are devoted to the rudiments of political economy. There is scarcely a proposition therein contained which is not subject to some qualification or limitation, arising out of special circumstances, or due to causes not mentioned in the text. Want of space has made the exclusion of many subjects unavoidable, and the author is perfectly conscious of the great gaps which result from a failure to refer to such questions as "currency," "exchange," "population," &c. But to those who desire to make a special study of political economy many exhaustive treatises on these matters are open. The object of the present volume is to show by simple examples what is the nature of economic laws, and to point out that their effect upon our lives is great and far-reaching.

No attempt has been made to apply strict definitions. On many of the important points of economical science the definitions of the various experts differ. It is not, however, necessary to settle the exact claims of the respective disputants before attempting to speak about the subject matter of their controversies.

The chapters in the present book devoted to "Trades Unions" and "Co-operative Societies" have received the approval of persons who are recognised as high authorities with respect to the aim and constitution of those important bodies; and special acknowledgments are due to these gentlemen for the valuable help they have given. Throughout the book it has been the special aim of the author to lay down as correctly as possible those rules of public duty and those maxims of wise public action which are accepted by honourable men of all creeds and all parties in the State.

A century ago the Government of this country was practically conducted by a small and special class, the members of which, whatever may have been their disqualifications, were at any rate educated from their earliest youth in the theory and practice of the difficult art of government. The worst of them had learnt to understand, and the best of them had learnt to display, the civic virtues which make a nation great. Now that the small class which nominated Pitt and Fox, Burke and Wilberforce, Lord Ellenborough and Lord North, has given way to, or rather has been swallowed up by, an electorate of over four millions, the need for education in matters of public duty has certainly not grown less than before.

It has, however, been assumed, somewhat too lightly, that the one art and mystery which can be advantageously undertaken without any special knowledge or training, is that of governing a great country. Seven years' apprenticeship is considered as barely sufficient to qualify a man to make a pair of shoes, but seven days' preparation is too often considered superfluous in order to enable the same individual to deal with the most formidable and intricate questions concerning the welfare of his country.

It is in the hope that it may prove a useful, though small, contribution to the great literature which must ere long be created for the instruction of the new rulers of the British Empire, that the present volume is laid before the public.

H. O. A. F.

CONTENTS

PART III
HOW TO LIVE UNDER THE LAW

PART IV
WORK AND WORKERS

CHAPTER I

INTRODUCTORY

THE LAWS WE LIVE UNDER

I

Why we ought to know the Law

"Every one is supposed to know the law of England." That is what the law-books tell us. Unfortunately, whatever the law-books may say, it is certain that very few people indeed do really know the law of England, and to pretend that every one knows it, is of course quite absurd. What is meant, however, by the lawyers, is something very different from this. What they really mean is that no one is to be excused for breaking the law merely because he is ignorant of it. And certainly if this be the case, it is advisable that every Englishman should try and learn something of the law which he is bound to obey, and which he may be punished for breaking.

Two Kinds of Law

There are, however, other laws, which are not the laws of England, but which it is equally important to know, and even more dangerous to break. These are the **Laws of Nature and of Reason.**

I want in this book to tell you something both about the laws of England which you are bound to obey, and about the laws of nature and reason which you are bound to obey also. But first I want to make quite clear what I mean by the words I have used.

The Law of the Land

By the laws of England I mean those rules and regulations which from time to time have been agreed upon by those who have governed our country, and which have for the most part been written down in charters and in Acts of Parliament. It is easy enough to understand the nature of these laws, and though every one does not perhaps know the punishments which are fixed for those who break them, still it is in the power of any one to find out, if he wishes, exactly what is the punishment which the law allows, and which can never be exceeded.

How to Learn it

For instance, the law of England says that every parent must educate his children or send them to school when they are of school age, and that if he does not do so he must be punished. Nearly everybody knows that this is the law, and nearly every one obeys the rule because it is the law. Everybody, however, does not know exactly the words of the law, or where it is to be found; but any one who wishes to see for himself, can, if he chooses, find and read the actual words of the Act of Parliament in which the rule is laid down, and can learn exactly the punishment which may be inflicted upon those who break it.

So, you see, it is not hard to understand what is meant by the law of England. But it is not quite so easy to understand what is meant by the laws of Nature and of Reason. It is worth while trying to understand, however, because it is even more dangerous to act contrary to these laws than to act contrary to the laws of England.

The Laws of Nature

When we talk of the laws of nature, what is it exactly that we mean? We say that by the law of nature there are 365 days in the year, or twenty-eight days in the month. We say that by the law of nature the tides rise and fall upon our shores.

What is it that we mean when we speak in this way? We mean that by noticing what actually happens under our eyes, we have been able to find out that the months and the years come round at certain fixed times; that the tides rise and fall at certain fixed intervals, and having found out that these things take place not once nor twice, but thousands of times in the same way, we have declared that the changes in each case are governed by a law in which there is no alteration.

We all know that the earth goes round the sun in 365 days, or one year, and so certain are we of the correctness of this law, and so sure are we that what took place last year will take place again next year and the year after and for years to come, that astronomers are able to look forward and to tell you in what position the earth will be ten years, or twenty years, or a hundred years hence.

How to Learn them, and
Why they must be Learnt

Sometimes it is a long time before these great natural laws are found out, and it is only by careful and patient study that we are enabled to discover them. But day by day we are finding out more and more of the secrets of nature, and day by day we are learning how complete and wonderful is the order which governs all things around us.

It is most important that men should study the laws of nature, in order that they may not waste their time in struggling against them. It is only when we do not know the law that we fight against it, and we always suffer in the long run for doing so.

When we know the law, we submit to it, and try to make use of it.

II

A Lesson from the Brook

A brook flows from the mountain down to the river, and the river flows down to the sea, and not all the power in the world will prevent the brook flowing down. Down, down it will go till its waters mingle with the waters of the sea. Block it up with a wall a hundred feet high, but still the stream will flow on, and will rise and rise against the wall till it rises to the top, then it will flow over it, and once more it will go, down, down to the sea.

Turn the stream along the mountain side, and dig new channels for it. The water will run in the new channels, it is true; you may turn the stream from its old bed, but it will only run down, down to the river, and down to the sea.

By the law of nature the stream will run down, and the strongest man cannot stop it. But if he be a wise man, though he cannot alter the law, he will know how to make use of it, and he will turn the law to his own advantage. He will build a dam across the stream, and will hold up the water till it is strong enough to turn his mill-wheel, and as it follows the natural law and runs down to the sea, it will grind his corn or weave his wool. He will dig channels for the stream along the hillside, and as it runs he will turn it into numbers of little trenches which will water his fields and make his pastures green and fertile.

Whenever men have learnt the laws of nature they are usually sensible enough not to fight against them. Sometimes, however, they do not know what these laws are, and because they do not know them they fight vainly against a power which they cannot possibly overcome. Nobody tries to make water run up-hill, but people often attempt to do things which are really not a whit more possible, simply because they do not know that they are fighting against the laws of nature.

III

Thor in the Land of the Giants

In the old Norwegian fairy tales we read a story of the great God Thor, which I shall tell you, because, though it is only a fairy tale, it will serve as a parable, or example, to explain what I want to teach you in this chapter.

Thor was one of the greatest of the old Norse gods, and he was famous above all others for his mighty strength. One day, as he was wandering forth on his travels, Thor came to the city of Jötenheim, in the land of the giants. Now, between the gods and the giants there was always rivalry and war, and Thor therefore knew that he was among enemies.

Utgard Loki, the king of the giants, ordered the stranger to be brought before him, and when he saw that Thor was smaller than any of his own subjects he laughed contemptuously at him, calling him a mere stripling. "We have heard much of your strength," said the king: "let us see what a boy like you can do, and then we shall know the worth of this boasting."

Confident in his great strength, Thor consented to make whatever trial Utgard Loki should command. "Here, then," said the king, "is my drinking-horn; pledge me in it; but thou must needs drink deep, for naught but a good drinker will drain it in a single draught." Thor put the horn to his lips and drank a deep, deep draught, but when he looked into the horn he saw that it was still all but full. Again he drank, and still the liquor stood high in the horn. He tried yet a third time, a longer pull than ever, but in vain. He threw the horn from him in despair. The giant and his fellows laughed scornfully at the discomfited god.

"Perhaps," said the king, "there is yet some other task less hard to perform and better suited to thy strength. See, here is my cat; try and lift it from the floor. It is an easy matter, in which we exercise our children here." A great grey cat sprang into the room, and Thor, putting his hand underneath her, strained and tugged with his uttermost strength to raise her up. In vain. With all his efforts he only succeeded in lifting one paw from the ground.

Again the giants laughed loud and long, and Thor, maddened by his failures, called upon any one present to try a match with him in wrestling, for never yet had his strength failed him in a bout. "I see none here," said the king, looking round, "who would not think it beneath him to wrestle with so small a man; but thou shalt see what thou canst do against my old nurse, Elli."

A very aged, toothless woman was brought into the hall, and Thor struggled with her for the mastery; but ere long he was forced upon his knee, and, owning himself beaten, he sullenly gave up his attempt to fight against powers for which even his great strength was plainly no match.

Next day, before Thor left the city, Utgard Loki sent for him, and, crestfallen and disheartened, the god presented himself before the king of the giants. "Tell me now," said the king, "hast thou not learnt a lesson of humility, and wilt thou not now acknowledge that with all thy boasted strength there are men, nay, that there are even old women, who are thy superiors?"

"I own," answered Thor, "that I have been fairly worsted, and that shame has overtaken me; yet have I done all that lay in my power, and I grieve that the mighty men of Utgard should so despise me and mock at me."

"Nay, then," said the king, "I will tell thee the truth. It is we who have reason to tremble, it is we who stand ashamed before thy mighty strength. Yesterday thy contest was not against us, but against others, whom the power of magic alone hid from thine eyes. The bottom of the horn from which thou drankest was set in the deep sea, and with thy mighty draught the tides along the shores of the ocean receded far below their usual limits.

"That cat which thou wouldest have lifted was none other than the great serpent, which circles the deep foundations of the solid earth. When, with a strength unknown to man, thy hand raised one of its vast paws, the earth trembled, and the giants of Utgard were themselves seized with fear.

"The grey-haired old nurse who brought thee to thy knee was Old Age, against whom none can wrestle but in vain. Go from this city, I beg thee, and return not again, and know well that it is not in Jötenheim that thou art despised, or that men fail to acknowledge thy strength."

The Moral of the Story

This story is a parable, and teaches us a lesson which should not be forgotten. The lesson it teaches is shortly this: that the strongest man or the strongest nation strives in vain against the laws of nature and reason. It therefore becomes necessary to study these laws, and to find out what they are, in order that we may work with and not against them.

We are none of us likely to try and dry up the ocean, or to shake the foundations of the earth, but many men through ignorance have tried to do things just as impossible, only because they did not see how strong a power they were fighting against.

You will easily understand how necessary it is that we should try to learn something of these laws, in order that we may not waste our time and strength in fighting against them.

Two Kinds of Law

I have tried to explain to you what is meant by natural laws—they are the rules which our experience and our observation have led us to believe are always observed in nature.

Now you will see what are the two kinds of law about which I wish to speak to you in this book. In the first place, there are the LAWS OF ENGLAND, or as they are sometimes called, the LAWS OF THE LAND; and, secondly, there are the LAWS OF NATURE AND OF REASON.

In the next chapter I shall tell you something about the law of the land, what it is, and why we ought to obey it.

SUMMARY

THE LAWS WE HAVE TO OBEY

1. As we are bound to obey the Law, and may be punished for breaking it, it is wise to learn what the Law is.

2. There are two kinds of Law which we must obey: the LAWS OF THE LAND, and the LAWS OF NATURE AND OF REASON.

3. Even though we cannot alter the Law, we can make use of it.

4. The Law of the Land may be learnt from books. The Laws of Nature and Reason are learnt by experience and observation.

Part I

THE LAW OF THE LAND

"I KNOW NO HUMAN BEING EXEMPT FROM THE LAW. THE LAW IS THE SECURITY OF THE PEOPLE OF ENGLAND; IT IS THE SECURITY OF EVERY PERSON THAT IS GOVERNED, AND OF EVERY PERSON THAT GOVERNS."   *Burke.*

CHAPTER II

THE NEED FOR LAW

IV

The Story of the "Bounty"

In the year 1789 an English ship named the *Bounty* sailed for the Pacific. It happened that there was much ill-feeling between the captain, who was called Bligh, and several of his crew. One day a party of the sailors, headed by an officer of the name of Fletcher Christian, broke out into open mutiny. They entered the captain's cabin fully armed, seized the captain himself, and put him and his friends into a little boat belonging to the ship, and then cast the boat adrift on the wide ocean.

After long and painful sufferings the captain and his companions succeeded in reaching the coast of Australia, whence they were finally brought back safely to England. Meanwhile the mutineers, with Christian at their head, went through many adventures and many dangers.

Some of them landed on the island of Tahiti, and at length a party of nine of them, including Christian, made their way to the little island known as Pitcairn

THE MUTINEERS CASTING CAPTAIN BLIGH ADRIFT

Island, in the midst of the South Pacific Ocean.[1] They took with them some of the natives from Tahiti, and among them several women who became the wives of the mutineers.

A Tiny Country

Here, then, was a little colony of about forty people living on a tiny island in the middle of the ocean, a thousand miles from the nearest land. The island itself was three miles long and a mile broad, and the whole population was smaller than that of the smallest English village.

You must remember that the chief people in this little population had come to be where they were through a shameful mutiny, and had acquired their new possession by breaking the laws which it was their duty to obey. It was perhaps for these reasons that they thought that the lawlessness which had succeeded so well in the past would serve them equally well in the future.

The Fruit of Lawlessness

Whatever may have been the reason for their conduct, they decided that it was better and easier to live without law and without rule than to make and obey any law whatever. Each man did what he pleased, without considering the claims of those among whom he lived.

We can hardly wonder at this. "Surely," they might

---

[1] On arriving at Pitcairn Island the mutineers removed all that they required from the *Bounty*, and then set fire to her.

have said, "it is possible for twenty or thirty people, living like Robinson Crusoe on a desert island in the middle of the ocean, to get on without rules and laws."

But it was not possible, as experience very soon showed. Each day a fresh quarrel broke out among the mutineers, and not only did they quarrel among themselves, but, by their violence and cruelty, they soon became the cause of quarrels and acts of violence among the Tahitians whom they had brought with them. Ere long some violent death overtook nearly every one of the Englishmen, till out of nine who had landed on the island two only were left alive, while out of the seven who had gone one only had died a peaceable death.

The Need for Law

Then it was that the two survivors, Edward Young and Alexander Smith,[2] began to find out that even in such a tiny country as theirs some law and rule were required. Terrified, no doubt, by the fate of their companions, and freed, too, from the bad influence of some of them, the two remaining Englishmen determined to turn over a new leaf. They set to work to instruct themselves, and to instruct those who were with them, in the plain rules of a Christian and civilised life.

During the years which the mutineers had been on the island, several children had been born, and were now growing up. The population of the little island was

---

[2] Alexander Smith was afterwards better known as John Adams.

increasing. It soon became clear that unless some laws were made as to how the land of the island should be divided, disputes would arise as to the share which each person should have. John Adams therefore divided the land into portions, giving so much to each family, and laying down the rule that on the death of any person his land should be divided into regular shares.

Of course, in order that Adams should be able to lay down these rules and compel others to obey them, it was necessary that he should receive some real authority. The islanders, however, soon saw the advantages of being properly governed, and they readily submitted to John Adams, and obeyed the rules he made for their advantage.

From this time forward the history of the mutineers of the *Bounty* becomes a very bright one. Far from all the great wars which at that time were disturbing Europe, they lived on peaceably and in order. John Adams instructed them in the truths of the Bible, and they learnt to live in obedience, not only to its words, but to its spirit.

PITCAIRN ISLAND

The Fruit of Law and Order

In 1849 Pitcairn Island was visited by a British ship of war, the *Pandora*, and this is what the captain says of this little colony which sprang from the lawless and cruel mutiny of the *Bounty*:— "I cannot but add my testimony to those who have gone before me as to the excellent moral and religious character of these people. Evil and crime seem unknown amongst them."

In 1856 the population had grown so much that the island was no longer able to provide its inhabitants with food, and, by the help of our Government and of many well-wishers in England, the whole people were moved to a larger and more fertile home in Norfolk Island, and there they and their descendants live to this day.

What the Story teaches us

From this story of the mutiny of the *Bounty* there is a lesson to be learnt. This lesson is that where men and women have to live and work together, however small may be their number, and however simple their wants, there must be some sort of government, some sort of law which all will recognise and obey.

Without law and without obedience the mutineers made their beautiful island even more dangerous and more disorderly than the ship which they had deserted. When once order, arrangement, and obedience were put in the place of lawlessness and selfishness, the little island began to prosper, and the people who lived on it to become happy and contented.

And what the descendants of the mutineers found to be true on Pitcairn Island, has been found to be true in every country in the world, at every period in history. Wherever we look, we shall find that no sooner have men and women begun to live together than they have begun also to lay down rules and regulations, and to give power to persons specially chosen to see that these rules and regulations are carried out.

V

Human Tigers

In every nation we find these rules and regulations, and we call them LAWS. The only exception to this truth is in the case of perfectly savage peoples, who are scarcely raised above the beasts among whom they live.

Travellers, for instance, tell us of some of the hill tribes of India, who know no law and obey no authority; if they have a dispute, instead of settling it, they separate, and go different ways; nor will they even live together, but, as they themselves say, "they are like tigers—two cannot dwell in one den," and they have their huts, therefore, scattered singly or in groups of two or three.

Here you have an instance of human beings living altogether without law or order, and you see that they themselves can find nothing better to compare themselves to than the wild beasts of the forest in which they live.

So true is it that without law and order, men become no better than wild animals.

The Growth of Law

The moment a people begins to become civilised, it will begin to make laws and regulations for itself. Among people who have very few wants and very few occupations, we usually find few and very simple laws. When, however, their wants increase and their occupations multiply, so also will their laws have to be increased in number and in exactness, in order to meet all the cases which may arise.

Laws on Pitcairn Island

For instance, on Pitcairn Island very few laws were necessary. Everybody lived by cultivating the land and by keeping cows and pigs. It was necessary, therefore, to make rules as to how the land should be divided for cultivation, and also how much of the land which was not cultivated should be given up to the owner of each cow or pig.

Then, later on, when the inhabitants began to get things from the English ships which touched at the island, and to supply the crew in return with fresh water and provisions, it became necessary to decide how much each person should give in order to obtain the articles which were needed for the common good. Rules had to be made laying down the quantity of yams,[3] or fruit, or pork, which each one was to bring, and the amount of work which each was to do in loading or unloading the ship. Such simple rules as these became the laws of the island. The wants and occupations of the people were few; the laws, therefore, were few also.

[3] Sweet potatoes.

Laws in England

But let us turn from Pitcairn Island to a great country like England, and you will see at once that the case is very different. Suppose a railway has to be made from one town to another, it will have to go through the property of a great many people, and if any of the people to whom the property belongs refuse to sell their ground to the railway, the line would never be made; and a law therefore has to be passed, giving the railway company the right to take the property, which does not belong to it, even against the will of the owners of the property.

CANNON STREET SIGNAL-BOX, LONDON

But of course that would be very unfair, if the land were not paid for, and so another law has to be made to settle how much the railway company must pay for the land, and how the price to be paid is to be decided. But that is not nearly all, for no sooner is the railway made than it becomes necessary to settle how it is to be safely worked, and more laws have to be made providing for proper signals to be used, and proper brakes, and for compelling the railway company to put proper fences along the sides of the line.

And even that is not the end of it, for while laws have to be made for the benefit of the people who use the railway on one side, on the other side the railway company itself must be protected by law from those who wish to use it wrongly; for instance, they must have a right to make people pay for their tickets, to make them obey necessary rules and regulations, and to prevent interference with the signals and points, and so on. Thus it will be seen that out of the making of one railway alone there springs up a necessity for many different laws, none of which were required in Pitcairn Island.

And what is true in this instance is true in many others, namely, that *in proportion as the wants and occupations of a people increase, so the necessity for fresh laws and rules will increase also.*

SUMMARY

THE NEED FOR LAW

1. Civilised men cannot live without law.

2. Those who live without law are uncivilised.

3. In proportion as the wants and occupations of a people increase, so will the necessity for fresh laws and regulations increase also.

CHAPTER III

HOW LAWS ARE MADE, AND WHY WE SHOULD OBEY THEM

VI

Two Ways of Winning Obedience to Law

THE laws of a country may be imposed upon the people in two ways—by *force* or by *consent*. In old times, when the government of England was in the hands of the king, or of a few great nobles only, the laws were sometimes made and carried out by force, and against the will of the people who had to obey them. These laws depended upon FORCE.

On the other hand, there are some laws which depend altogether upon the CONSENT of the people, and which everybody agrees to obey. But by far the greater number of our laws depend both upon force and upon the consent of the people. Those who agree and consent to the laws submit to them willingly, those who disagree with them or break them are compelled to submit to them by force.

By Force

Of course, it is no use having a law unless it is to be obeyed, and power must therefore be given to those who have made the law to punish those who break it, and if they resist, to use force against them. In the early times of which I have spoken to you, the king and the nobles were really more powerful than the people over whom they ruled. Their strong castles, their good weapons, and their great possessions enabled them to enforce their will upon the rest of the people, even though the latter far outnumbered them.

By Consent

Nowadays, when all the people of England have the same equal rights, and when the old power of the nobles has long been forgotten, a great change has taken place. It is still the most powerful who make the laws and who enforce obedience to them, only now that the right of governing has been taken away from a few and given to all the people alike, it is plain that the strength and power which once belonged only to a very few have now been given to the whole people. If all the people of England agree upon a law and determine that it shall be obeyed, it will be impossible for anybody to think of successfully resisting their will by force.

The Old Plan

Sometimes, however, it happens that there is a difference of opinion as to what law it is wisest to make. Formerly when there was such a difference of opinion men very often fought to decide which way should be chosen, and waited until a battle was fought and one side was victorious over the other before they would consent to accept the new law.

Thus "Magna Charta" itself, upon which the liberties of Englishmen are founded, was only won from King John by the Barons after long and hard fighting, and there is not one of the sixty-three rules which the Charter contains which was not a matter of dispute and conflict between the King and the Barons, and which was not finally settled by the sword instead of by argument, by voting, or by Act of Parliament.

The very law which forbids a king or queen of England to take taxes from the people save by the lawful consent of the people themselves was gained in this way by the sword.[4]

And the New

But now we have found a better and a wiser plan. Formerly it was often impossible to know which side in the country was really the stronger, for the duty of making laws and carrying them out was entrusted only to a few, and there were no means of finding out what the whole people of the country really wished, and which side was in fact the stronger; and the result was, as I have told you, that terrible wars were sometimes fought before the question was decided.

Now, however, we have no need to act in this way.

---

[4] These are the words as they appear:—"No scutage or aid shall be levied in our kingdom save by the Common Council of the kingdom."

Whenever laws have to be made for the whole country, Parliament is called together, and the opinion of the members of the House of Commons is asked before the law is made. Now, the members of the House of Commons, as you know, are elected by the whole of the people of this country, and if the greater number, or, as it is usually called, the MAJORITY of the House of Commons give their consent to a new law, or to an alteration in an old one, it is then fair to say that what the majority of the House of Commons wishes, the majority of the people by whom they are chosen wish also.

In this way it is easy to see which party is the stronger; and the smaller party, or the MINORITY, instead of fighting battles and getting beaten, submit to the will of what they know to be the stronger party. By this means much confusion and suffering are avoided, and quiet and orderly government is obtained.

In this country we have found this plan works so well that most people are content to submit to the laws made by the majority, even though they themselves may have been opposed to the laws before they received the approval of Parliament.

VII

An Example

Up to the year 1870 there was no law in this country compelling parents to send their children to school. In that year a Bill was brought into Parliament, the object of which was to set up schools all over the country and to provide schooling at the public expense for all those children whose teaching was not otherwise paid for.

When this Bill was brought into Parliament a great number of people opposed it and tried to prevent it becoming law. They did not all oppose it for the same reasons. Some thought that if the Bill were passed the teaching which would be given would be of a bad kind, others thought that the expense would be too great, and some opposed the Bill because they thought that it would put too much power into the hands of those whom they distrusted or from whom they differed. All these different parties joined together and fought hard to prevent the Bill getting through Parliament, for they honestly thought that if it were to become law it would do harm.

However, it appeared at last that the majority of Parliament and the majority of the people were in favour of the Bill, and in the end it became part of the law of the land, which every one was bound to obey.

What has happened since? Have those who objected to the Act resisted it ever since it has been a part of the law? Certainly not. Many of them, no doubt, still dislike some parts of it, but no one is found to resist or to advise people to break it.

On the contrary, very many of those who disagreed most with the law have since made up their minds, not only to submit to it, but have themselves set to work to make the best possible use of it. By accepting the law which they could not prevent, and by making the best use of it, they have done far more to gain their objects and to do the good they wanted to do, than they could possibly have accomplished by trying to resist or interfere with the law.

A Noble Lady

The history of the Education Act reminds me of a story which is told of a rich lady living in London. This lady had a large and beautiful house not very far from one of the great parks. One side of the house looked over a garden. There was no road close to it, and it therefore enjoyed that great blessing which is so rare in London—it was quiet and undisturbed by the noise of the endless carriages.

But it became necessary, for the good of the public and for the convenience of the thousands who use the London streets, that a new road should be cut close to the lady's house.

It was plain that when the road was cut, her peace and quiet would be gone for ever, and rather than lose this treasure the lady offered to spend a large sum of money, amounting to thousands of pounds, to resist the plan and to compel the road-makers to choose another direction. However, her efforts were in vain; the road was made, and with it came the din of the carriages.

Then the lady did a very wise and good thing. "I have not succeeded," she said, "in preventing this disturbance of my comfort, though I was willing to pay a large sum for the purpose, but now that the thing is done, and I cannot help it, I will do my best to make the work a success. I will give the same sum which

I intended to spend in opposing the road, towards extending, widening, and improving it. In that way, if I lose, as I certainly shall, the public, at any rate, will gain."

Here is a good example for all those who honestly oppose a law which is passed in spite of them. Prevent it if you can, but if you cannot, try and make the best possible use of it when it is made. That is indeed how a good citizen should act.

It is fortunate that Englishmen are as ready to obey a law when it is once made as they are to prevent a law being made which they do not like or approve of; for you must remember that, unless people were to submit in this way to the will of the majority in Parliament, there would be only one other way of settling questions at all, and that would be to go back to the old barbarous fashion of fighting and making war, which has done so much harm and caused so much suffering in the past.

VIII

How to get a Law Altered

Of course, if anybody thinks a law unjust or harmful, he ought not simply to remain quiet and do nothing to get it altered or done away with. On the contrary, he ought to use every effort in order to persuade other people to share his view and to help him in obtaining his object. By-and-by, if he is active and persevering, and if the reasons he gives are strong enough to convince his neighbours, he will win over friends to his side, and, in the end, he may succeed in getting the majority of the people to support him.

Then there will be no need to fight and to shed blood in order to get the law changed, but it will only be necessary to send to Parliament a majority of members who are of his own way of thinking, and they will alter or put an end to the law in just the same orderly and quiet way in which those who went before them first made it.

Why the Law is Obeyed

You will see, therefore, what I meant by saying that the law in our country depends partly upon *force* and partly upon *consent*. The greater number of people obey the law because they themselves made it and because they approve of it. *In their case the law rests upon consent.*

A smaller number, who do not approve of the law, still obey it partly by consent, because they are wise enough to agree to rules which are approved of by the majority, and partly because they know that, whether they like the law or not, those who have made the law are strong enough to compel obedience to it.

In the case of the smaller number, or minority, the law rests therefore *partly upon consent and partly upon force.* For instance, there are some persons who do not like sending their children to school, but who nevertheless do send them every day, as they are bound to do by the law. Many of those who object obey the law because now that it is the law they feel that it is their duty, as good citizens, to obey it. In their case their obedience is owing to *consent.*

Others there are who obey the law only because they know that if they do not they will be punished by fine or imprisonment. In their case the law rests upon *force* and is obeyed through fear. And, lastly, it must not be forgotten that there is often a small number of persons who do not consent to obey the law at all, but who are made to do so by force, and punished by force if they break the law.

The law says that people shall not steal; and there is so little difference of opinion about its being a bad thing to steal, that the law against it is supported by the consent of nearly everybody in the country. There are, however, as you know, people who try to make their living by stealing, and who, though they know quite well what the law is, intentionally break it. It is necessary to make such persons as this obey the law by force, and accordingly, as you know, those who are found guilty of stealing or of wilfully breaking the law are punished by being put in prison or by being fined. THOSE WHO WILFULLY DISOBEY THE LAW MUST BE PUNISHED.

SUMMARY

OBEDIENCE TO THE LAW

1. Laws are enforced by (*a*) consent; (*b*) force; (*c*) partly by consent and partly by force.

2. The Law must be obeyed until it is altered.

3. The Law can only be altered by Parliament.

CHAPTER IV

HOW GOOD CITIZENS SHOULD HONOUR THE LAW

IX

Laws we Suffer from

You will perhaps think that I have told you a good deal about laws and law-making which is not likely ever to be of much service to you; but it is a mistake to suppose that the reasons which I have given you do not concern every one of us.

It very often happens in such a great country as our own that the actual laws which have been made and by which we are governed press very hardly upon particular people, and cause much discontent and suffering. Those who suffer and those who are discontented are naturally very ready to complain of that which appears to them harsh and unjust, and they are even ready sometimes to do violent and unlawful things with the hope of bettering their condition.

When any one is tempted to act in this way it would be useful for him to remember some of the facts I have just told you—how laws are made and why they should be obeyed.

It is easy enough for any man to say, "Here is a law from which I suffer inconvenience and loss; it must be a bad law, and I have the right to resist and to disobey it." But if he did say this he would be wrong.

How John Hampden did his Duty

A good example of the way in which an honourable and good citizen should behave is furnished by the story of JOHN HAMPDEN. John Hampden was member of Parliament for the county of Buckinghamshire in the reign of Charles I. In the year 1636 the King, being in want of money, tried to levy a tax called *ship money,* a tax which had not been voted by Parliament, and to the collection of which Parliament had not consented.

The King and those who supported him declared that, by an ancient right, the King was at liberty to make his subjects pay this tax if he chose, and that Parliament had nothing to do with the matter. John Hampden, on the other hand, believed that the King had no right to the money unless Parliament voted that he should have it, and when the tax-collectors came to his house he refused to pay.

"You are compelled by law," said the tax-collectors, "to pay the money." "No," replied Hampden, "the law is against you, and the demand you make upon me is illegal." You must notice that Hampden did not say, "The law is a bad law, and I refuse to obey it." What he did say was, "Your version of the law is wrong, and until you prove it to be the law, I refuse to pay."

JOHN HAMPDEN

Hampden Appeals to the Law

The next thing that happened was that the case between the King and John Hampden was tried before the judges, for it was the duty of the judges then, as it is now, to decide what the law really was. Hampden was prosecuted for non-payment of ship money. Twelve judges sat to hear the case, and for twelve days Hampden and his friends argued in favour of their cause.

At last the decision was given. Eight of the judges, anxious to please the King and win favour in the future, decided against Hampden; four were in his favour. The law, therefore, was decided to be against him. What did Hampden do? Did he refuse to recognise the decision of the judges? Did he attempt to resist by force the officers of the King?

Hampden Obeys the Law

Nothing of the kind. He knew that the decision was unjust, and that some, at any rate, of the judges who decided against him did so on bad and dishonest grounds, but he remembered that he himself had appealed to the law, and, now that he found that the law was against him, he submitted to it, and paid the tax which he had at first refused.

Do not suppose, however, that Hampden was content to let matters rest here. He knew perfectly well that though it was his duty to submit to the law until it was altered, yet that it was no less his duty to work with all his might to alter the law, if it were a bad one, and to put a just one in its place.

Among all the men who took part in fighting for the cause of good government in the stormy times of the Rebellion, no man took a braver or wiser part than John Hampden. At last, when it appeared plainly that the King himself and his advisers were determined to break the law rather than submit to Parliament, Hampden himself felt obliged to take up arms and fight for what he believed to be right. He was killed in a skirmish at *Chalgrove Field* in July, 1643.

This example of John Hampden shows us exactly what is the duty of a wise and patriotic man. It was Hampden's right, and in a similar case it is ours, to object as strongly as possible to an unjust law; it was Hampden's right, and it is ours, to take every step to find out whether what is done be really in accordance with the law or not. It was Hampden's duty, and it would be ours in a similar case, when it appeared that the law was against us, to submit to the decision of the judges until, by proper and orderly means, the unjust law had been altered.

X

Armed Resistance to Law

Of course, I do not forget that in many cases, both in this country and abroad, men have rebelled against unjust and oppressive laws, and have taken up arms against those who sought to put the law into force. There are many examples of this, some of which you will remember to have read in your histories.

To begin with, there is the case of the friends of that very John Hampden of whom I have just been speaking. You know that in the year 1642 the members of the Parliamentary party took up arms against King Charles I, and finally defeated him, took him prisoner, tried him, and put him to death.

In that case, however, it must not be forgotten that most of those who opposed the King did so on the ground that Charles himself had broken the law of England by acting without the consent and against the advice of his Parliament, and most of

CHARLES I

them declared and believed that they were fighting on behalf of the law, and not against it.

But there are many other instances in which laws have been resisted by force, simply because they were unjust and cruel, or because they appeared to be so to those who took up arms against them.

King Henry of Navarre

Such was the case of the French "Huguenots" or Protestants, who, in the reign of Henry III of France, and in the time of our Queen Elizabeth, took up arms against the King on account of the harsh and oppressive laws which he tried to put in force against their religion. It was during this war that the battle of Ivry was fought, which Macaulay has made so famous in his poem,

Many of you, I am sure, have read the poem, and will remember how King Henry of Navarre,[5] the leader of the Protestant army, gave the word to his troops to follow the white plume in his helmet into the thick of the battle.

Here are some of the lines of Macaulay's poem, which may perhaps help you to remember this example. The verses describe the scene before the beginning of the battle:—

"The King is come to marshal us in all his armour drest,
And he has bound a snow-white plume upon his gallant crest.

[5] King Henry of Navarre became afterwards King Henry IV of France. He changed the form of his religion and became a Roman Catholic, but throughout his reign he treated the Protestants with the greatest justice and favour.

He looked upon his people, and a tear stood in his eye;
He looked upon the traitors and his glance was stern and high.
Right graciously he smiled on us, as rolled from wing to wing,
Down all our line a deafening shout, 'God save our Lord
    the King!'
'And if my standard-bearer fall, as fall full well he may,
For never saw I promise yet of such a bloody fray,
Press where ye see my white plume shine amidst the ranks
    of war,
And be your oriflamme[6] to-day the helmet of Navarre.'

"Hurrah! the foes are moving. Hark to the mingled din
Of fife, and steed, and trump, and drum, and roaring culverin.[7]
The fiery Duke is pricking fast across St. André's plain,
With all the trusty chivalry of Guelders[8] and Almayne.[9]
'Now, by the lips of those ye love, fair gentlemen of France,
Charge for the golden lilies, upon them with the lance!'
A thousand spurs are striking deep, a thousand spears in rest,
A thousand knights are pressing close behind the snow-white
    crest,
And in they burst, and on they rushed, while like a guiding
    star,
Amidst the thickest carnage blazed the helmet of Navarre."

It would plainly be absurd to say that all those who
took part in such rebellions as this, or who at any time
resisted the law of the land by force of arms, were wrong
or wicked. On the contrary, we know that many of
them are held in high honour, and that their names
have been handed down as worthy of admiration by
their descendants.

---

[6] Oriflamme, the royal flag of France.
[7] Culverin, a small cannon.
[8] Guelders, the Dutchy of Guelders, now part of Germany.
[9] Almayne, Germany.

An Englishman's Way of Altering the Law

How, then, can it be true, as I told you in the beginning of this chapter, that it was the duty of every man to submit to the law until it was altered in a proper and lawful manner? The answer to this question is a simple one. In past times the people of the country had little or no voice in making the laws by which they were governed, and however much they disapproved of them they were quite unable to alter them.

Nowadays, however, every inhabitant of the United Kingdom who possesses a vote has the right to take part in making the laws; and not only has he this power, but, thanks to the freedom of speech which is now permitted to all, he is able to say anything that he pleases to persuade others to share his view, and to join with him in bringing about the alteration which he desires.

Civil War

It is, indeed, possible that the majority of the people who now possess the power that was formerly in the hands of kings or nobles may make as great mistakes and do things which are as unjust and oppressive as the kings and nobles who came before them.

In such a case it may possibly happen that those who suffer from such injustice and oppression may determine to resist by force the decision of Parliament, as their ancestors in times gone by resisted the decision of kings and nobles; but if they do so, and if they take upon them the terrible responsibility of shedding blood and breaking the law of the land in order to serve their own purposes, they ought to remember, and every one who encourages them ought to remember, that no law can ever be upheld unless those who break it are punished.

Those who in past times resisted the king were called *rebels,* and when they fought against the law they knew that they risked their own lives in doing so. And if a man who, by force of arms, resisted the king, when the king acted without the consent or approval of the whole people, was a rebel and worthy of punishment, how much more serious is the offence of a man who takes up arms against the majority of his countrymen, and who by so doing brings upon them the misery and shame of civil war!

The Punishment of a Rebel

A man who does such a thing, however strongly he may believe in his cause, and however positive he may be that he is in the right, must be fully prepared to take the consequences of what he does, and must remember that the law is bound to punish in the severest possible way those who, for whatever reason, try to set it aside and to resist it.

A man who takes up arms against the law of the land nowadays is as much a rebel as any one who fought against the king four or five hundred years ago, and he should understand that he takes his life in his hand, and that he may justly be made to pay the penalty of his offence with his life.

But let me say once more that, although it is possible that a time may come when men in this country will take up arms and rebel against the Government, it is very unlikely that, until some great change comes over our Parliament, those who act in such a way will be doing what is right or will deserve to escape the severest punishment.

XI

The "Many" and the "Few"

You must not think for a moment that those who are in the majority are always in the right, or that a thing is right because the majority approve of it. On the contrary, we know that many great truths have been taught to the world by men who at first were in a very small minority, and who had to face suffering, danger, and death in their efforts to persuade others of the truth of their belief. The Christian religion itself was for many years the faith of a very small number only, and those who taught it were few and despised. Its great founder, Christ Himself, "was despised and rejected of men."

It is not because the majority are always right that we are bound to submit to their will. It is because the experience of our past history has taught us that the best and most successful way of avoiding strife, and bloodshed, and discontent is to accept the will of the majority expressed, not by force of arms, but in an orderly and legal manner, by means of chosen representatives sitting in a Parliament where every one is free to speak as he chooses.

On the whole, our experience has taught us that it is better to submit for a time to laws which may be bad or insufficient, than to get rid of them by violence and force. Sometimes it is a long time before those who seek to alter and improve the law can get their way, and they are compelled to spend months and years in teaching the people how much better off they will be when the change has been made.

A Great Mistake

Thus, when laws were first made forbidding the employment of women and children in factories for more than a certain number of hours each day, many people were very angry that such rules should have been made. They declared it was cruel to the women and children to prevent them doing all the work they could get, they declared it would lower their wages, and that, moreover, it would very much diminish the quantity of goods which could be made in the factories.

They foretold, on the one hand, that the workers would suffer from starvation, and on the other, that the employers would be ruined by being prevented from getting the work they required done. So firmly did many people believe in these gloomy prophecies that they actually used violence to try and prevent the laws being passed, and they induced many of the workers to take part in riots and attacks upon those who favoured the change.

At last, however, the law was passed in spite of them, and gradually people began to see how good and useful a law it really was. Not only were the employers not ruined, but they got their work done better than before. Not only did the wages of the women and children not go down, but they became higher than before; the work they did was better and not worse than before.

Before long, no one was more grateful for the law than those who had been foremost in opposing it. And now everybody is agreed that it was a right and good thing to shorten the long hours of work which used to make the lives of hundreds and thousands of women and children a misery and a burden to them.

The very fact, however, that it has been so difficult to persuade the majority of the people to change their minds, is often a proof that it would have been unwise to make the change when it was first proposed, for though it is important that a law should be good and wise in itself, it is almost equally important that the majority of those who have to obey it should think it a good one.

The Duty of Law-Makers

I will give you also an example of the harm which may be done by keeping up a law after people have ceased to believe in its usefulness or justice. It will show you how careful those who make the laws ought to be to see that, as time goes and men's opinions alter, the laws by which men are to be governed are altered also, so that the law of the land may always receive respect and obedience.

The Harm Done by Bad Laws

At the end of the last century, and indeed at the beginning of the present, the law against certain classes of law-breakers was terribly severe. The punishment for stealing a sheep was death, the punishment for stealing a sum of over 40s. was death, and for many other offences, which, though wrong in themselves, would nowadays be considered very trifling, the punishment was death or transportation for life to some distant prison across the seas.

Now, such cruel punishments as these did harm in many ways. In the first place, it did harm to the whole people to become accustomed to see justice done by such bad means. Men who see an example of cruelty and carelessness for human life set by those in high places, and approved of by the law, are in danger of becoming themselves cruel and careless.

But this was not all. Another great evil sprang up which perhaps we should not at first have expected. Among those who were put upon the juries, whose duty it was to try men charged with stealing and other small offences, were many who felt, as we should feel now, that to sentence a fellow-creature to death for a fault of this kind was unjust, and indeed wicked.

Thinking as they did, they could not possibly help to bring about the death of the prisoners; but if once the prisoner were found guilty by the jury of having committed the crime with which he was charged, the judge was bound by the law, which he did not dare

45

disobey, to sentence him to be hanged. The only way, therefore, in which the jurymen could help the prisoner was to say that he was "not guilty," and this is what, in fact, they often did.

Now, though this was perhaps better than helping to bring about the prisoner's death, it was a very bad plan. In the first place, if the prisoner had really committed the offence for which he was being tried, the jurymen who declared that he was not guilty were saying what they knew to be untrue, and were breaking their oaths, by which they were bound to "well and truly try the issue between His Sovereign Lord the King and the prisoner at the bar, and a true verdict give according to the evidence."

Nor was this all: the prisoner who had broken the law not only escaped the punishment of death, but got off scot-free, without any punishment whatever, which was a bad thing in itself, and was a great encouragement to other evildoers to break the law, in the hope that they too might be found "not guilty" by another jury of the same way of thinking as the first. Here, then, were bad results all round, and all coming from the same cause, namely, that *the law was no longer in agreement with the feelings of the majority of those who had to obey it.*

XII

A Difficult Question

There is one case which often puzzles people very much, and which leads them to neglect some of the truths which have been referred to in this chapter.

You will often find people who, though they are ready enough to agree in a general way with those who say that the will of the majority ought to be obeyed, are nevertheless the first to act contrary to their own words as soon as they themselves suffer any inconvenience from a law which the majority have approved, but which they find inconvenient or unpleasant. It generally happens that those who make such a mistake as this do not look far enough. The old saying tells us of a man who walking through the forest declared he could not see the wood for the trees.

Scarlet Fever in the House

And so it is with people who do not try to look a little beyond their own particular interests, and to inquire whether what seems harsh and troublesome to them, may not be only a necessary part of a plan which has been made for the benefit of all.

Let me give an example which will show you exactly what I mean. It is the rule in almost all towns that whenever a case of infectious fever, such as small-pox or scarlet fever, breaks out in any house, the persons who live in the house should at once give notice to the officers who look after the public health. Directly these officers hear of the case of fever they go to the house and insist upon proper care being taken to prevent the infection spreading.

It often happens that, in order to make quite sure that the infection shall not be carried away to others, it is necessary to remove the sick person to a hospital, to burn the bedding and clothes which he has used, and to shut up the house altogether for a time. It is easy to see how inconvenient this may be to those who live in the house, especially if it be a shop or a place of business. Shutting up the house may often cause a great loss of money and trade to persons who themselves are quite free from illness, and who can ill afford to be deprived of the means of getting a livelihood.

For the Good of Others

And yet there can be no doubt that in taking every possible care, and in using the authority which the law gives them, the officers of health, or *"sanitary officers"* as they are called, are acting wisely and are doing their duty.

Nor can there be any doubt that those who suffer inconvenience and loss from the action of the sanitary officers will be doing very wrong if they complain, and still more if they try to resist the law, or to escape from the inconvenience to which they are put.

For of course it is a thousand times better that one or two or half-a-dozen persons should suffer loss, or even ruin, than that such terrible and fatal diseases as small-pox and scarlet fever should be spread throughout the country. Those who, without any fault on their part, are made to suffer in this way, will do wisely to remember these things, and to submit to a law which, though it bears hardly on them, is made for the good of all.

This is a very clear case, and I should think there are very few who would not acknowledge that it was their duty to submit without complaint to rules of the kind I have referred to.

But cases may arise in which people do not find it so easy to understand the reasons for the laws and regulations which seem oppressive. This is especially the case when those who suffer loss or inconvenience have not taken any pains to study the reasons for which laws are made, or to acquaint themselves with the real dangers which these laws are intended to guard against.

What the Corn-field Teaches us

It is wonderful how different the same thing may look from two different points of view. Stand in a field of corn, and look across it from corner to corner, all will be confusion—a sea of waving grain, without method or arrangement.

But let us change our position a little, and let us look at the same field from a different point of view. Immediately, instead of confusion, there will be method; instead of disorder, there will be arrangement; and on all sides we shall see the long straight lines of the furrows stretching away, and the corn-stems rising in regular rows, as far as the eye can reach.

ORDER AND DISORDER; OR, TWO WAYS OF LOOKING AT IT.

By looking at the field from a different point of view, we shall see at once that there were wisdom and reason in the minds of the plougher and the sower, and that we had only failed to see the proof of them because we had not looked at their work from the right point of view.

SUMMARY

THE CONSEQUENCE OF BREAKING THE LAW

1. The law must be obeyed even by those who suffer from it.

2. Those who wilfully break the law *must* be punished.

3. Now that the whole people make the law, any one who rebels against the law rebels against the whole people.

4. Those laws will be most readily obeyed which are approved by those who have to obey them.

5. Laws which are made for the good of many often bear hardly upon a few.

6. But it is the duty of the few to submit to them.

7. We sometimes condemn laws and call them hard only because we do not understand the reasons for them.

8. There is a right way and a wrong way of looking at most things; it is our business to find the right way.

Part II

THE LAWS OF NATURE AND REASON

"WE ARE PLACED HERE BELOW, NOT TO CREATE HUMAN NATURE, BUT TO CARRY IT FORWARD; . . . ALL THE ELEMENTS OF HUMAN ACTIVITY, INDIVIDUAL PROPERTY, RICHES, ETC., ARE IN THEMSELVES NEITHER GOOD NOR EVIL. WE SHOULD BLAME NONE OF THEM; WE SHOULD FIND OUT HOW TO DIRECT THEM ARIGHT." *Mazzini.*

CHAPTER V

THE LAW OF SUPPLY AND DEMAND

XIII

The Nature of the Law

I NOW want you to pay attention to another set of laws which concern us not less nearly than the laws of the land of which I have spoken.

These are the laws which govern the dealings of men with one another. You would think at first that in such matters as *buying and selling, working and wage-earning, spending and saving,* there were no fixed and certain rules, but that each man settled for himself what he would buy or sell, what work he would do or what wage he would accept, what he would save and what he would spend.

I want to show you that this is not so, but that, on the contrary, there are laws which affect all these matters very closely, and which have to be understood and observed no less than the other laws of which I spoke to you just now. Moreover, I want to point out to you that these laws are only the rules which experience and observation have taught us always prevail, and which we must make use of if we want to do good work.

When I have explained to you the nature of these laws you will see that it is most important to know them because, whether we like it or not, they will apply to us and to our work, and if we do not try and make use of them, and act in accordance with them, we shall be certain to be sufferers in the long run.

Why we Ought to Know them

Buying and selling, working and earning, saving and spending, must, as you all know, form a great part of the life of every one of us. There is no one so rich and no one so poor as not to have something to do with these matters. Most of us have a great deal to do with them.

Now, as I told you, every one of these matters is regulated by a law or by a number of laws which, if we choose, we can discover in whole or in part, and which we shall be wise to bear in mind whenever we buy and sell, work and earn wages, or employ others and pay them wages. Many a man has been made poorer and more unhappy because he himself or those who governed his country did not understand or did not pay attention to these laws. Much suffering has been removed and much happiness conferred by carefully studying these laws and wisely submitting to them.

XIV

Supply and Demand

The first of these laws of which I shall speak to you is the law of SUPPLY AND DEMAND.

The law which made the water of the brook flow down to the sea is the law of gravitation. We call it a law because wherever man has had the power to observe he has found that the rule is the same, and invariable. The law of which I am now going to speak is of quite another kind, but we have learnt to call it a law for just the same reason, that is, because wherever we have been able to study those things which the law applies to, we have found it to be the same and invariable.

The Law and the Breakfast-table

You will think it a strange thing to come down from talking about laws to such a simple thing as the breakfast-table, but it is just because the one has something to do with the other, and just because the great law of which I have been speaking does really concern our daily life, that I am going to give up a chapter to telling you about it.

What is the Price of a Pound of Tea?

What is the price of a pound of tea? You can give half-a-dozen answers to that question, which will all be right, for a pound of tea may cost ls. 6d., or 2s., or 3s., or sometimes as much even as 10s. And the next question is, Why does it cost ls. 6d., or 2s., or 3s., or whatever the price may be? There is a very plain answer

55

to that question, and there is a very good reason why it should cost just exactly what it does in fact cost, and no more and no less.

It is all a matter of rule and reason, and as the rules and reasons which fix the price of a pound of tea are exactly the same as those which fix the price of a ton of coals, or a sack of potatoes, a diamond necklace, an elephant, a railway ticket, a lesson on the fiddle, or of anything else which is bought and sold, it is very well worth our while to try and master a rule which will help us in so many cases.

"The price of any article is regulated by the law of supply and demand." That is the rule put quite shortly; but, of course, the rule does not help us much until we know exactly what it means. Let us try and understand it with the help of one or two examples.

A Great Demand

There are some things for which there is a great demand. If you want an example, try and hold your breath for half a minute, and you will soon see that the thing for which you have the greatest demand is a fresh supply of air in your lungs; and what is true of you is true of everybody else all over the world.

Everywhere there is a demand for air to breathe; everybody wants it in order to live; and yet if I were to ask you what you have to pay every time you open your mouth and take a long breath, and what the air you take into your lungs costs you, you would laugh at me; for, of course, you know very well that you have to pay nothing at all for the air you breathe.

The reason of this is, not that there is no demand for air—for, as I told you, everybody must have air in order to live—but because there is an endless supply of it. There is everywhere enough for all, and to be got only at the expense of opening your mouths. And therefore it is that we can put no price on the air we breathe.

XV

The Story of the Black Hole of Calcutta

But now let me tell you a story which will show you what I meant by saying that price is fixed by the law of supply and demand.

More than a century ago, when the rule of England in India was not firmly fixed, and when our countrymen were fighting against both the French and the native princes, a great disaster befell a number of Englishmen and women in the city of Calcutta. Surajah Dowlah, the Nabob or Viceroy of the great Province of Bengal, in which Calcutta is situated, suddenly marched an army into the town and besieged the fort by which it was protected.

Frightened by the stories of Surajah Dowlah's cruelty, the Governor of Calcutta fled from his post. The commander of the troops followed the shameful example. The fort was taken, and great numbers of the English fell into the hands of the conquerors. The Nabob seated himself with regal pomp in the principal hall of the Factory,[10] and ordered Mr. Holwell, the first in rank among the prisoners, to be brought before him. His Highness talked about the insolence of the English, and grumbled about the smallness of the treasure which he had found; but promised to spare their lives, and retired to rest. This is how Lord Macaulay tells the rest of the terrible story:—

A Terrible Crime

"Then was committed that great crime, memorable for its singular atrocity, memorable for the tremendous retribution by which it was followed. The English captives were left to the mercy of the guards, and the guards determined to secure them for the night in the prison of the garrison, a chamber known by the fearful name of the "Black Hole.""

"Even for a single European malefactor that dungeon would, in such a climate, have been too close and narrow. The space was only twenty feet square. The air-holes were small and obstructed. It was the summer solstice, the season when the fierce heat of Bengal can scarcely be rendered tolerable to natives of England by lofty halls and by the constant waving of fans. The number of the prisoners was 146.

"When they were ordered to enter the cell they imagined that the soldiers were joking, and, being in high spirits on account of the promise of the Nabob to spare their lives, they laughed and jested at the absurdity of the notion. They soon discovered their mistake. They

[10] Factory =the settlement in which the English merchants lived.

expostulated, they entreated, but in vain. The guards threatened to cut down all who hesitated. The captives were driven into the cell at the point of the sword, and the door was instantly shut and locked upon them.

A Night of Horror

"Nothing in history or fiction approaches the horrors which were recounted by the few survivors of that night. They cried for mercy, they strove to burst the door. Holwell, who, even in that extremity, retained some presence of mind, offered large bribes to the gaolers; but the answer was that nothing could be done without the Nabob's orders, that the Nabob was asleep, and that he would be angry if anybody woke him.

"Then the prisoners went mad with despair. They trampled each other down, fought for the places at the windows, fought for the pittance of water with which the cruel mercy of the murderers mocked their agonies, raved, prayed, implored the guards to fire among them. The gaolers in the meantime held lights to the bars, and shouted with laughter at the frantic struggles of their victims.

"At length the tumult died away in low gaspings and moanings. The day broke. The Nabob had slept off his debauch, and permitted the door to be opened; but it was some time before the soldiers could make a lane for the survivors, by piling up on each side the heaps of corpses. When at length a passage was made, twenty-three ghastly figures, such as their own mothers would not have known, staggered, one by one, out of the charnel-house. A pit was instantly dug. The dead bodies, 123 in number, were flung into it promiscuously, and covered up."

XVI

Such is the terrible story of the "Black Hole" of Calcutta. Now, there can be no doubt whatever that any one of these unhappy people would have given all the wealth he possessed for the power to breathe that fresh air which you are breathing now.

Why was this? Why was it that in one case so common a thing as air should have been worth a greater price than gold or diamonds, while in the other case no one should think of paying any price for it at all?

The answer is a simple one. It is that in the first case there was less air to be got than was required by those

GOVERNMENT HOUSE, CALCUTTA

who were imprisoned. In other words, the demand was very great and the supply was very small. In the other case, though there are a great many people wanting the fresh air, there is far more fresh air for them to breathe than they can ever possibly want. That is to say, although the demand is great, the supply is very much greater. Thus we shall find that, in all cases, the price of anything which is bought and sold will increase whenever the demand for it be large and the supply of it small.

A Costly Bit of Coal

Let us take three or four instances. Everybody knows that the price of diamonds is very high. As much as £135,000 has been paid for a single diamond.[11] What is it that makes the price of diamonds so high? It is not that the diamond itself is a very useful thing, for except as an ornament it is not very much used,[12] and, as for the stone itself, it is really only a little crystal, made up of the same carbon which forms the coals that we put upon the fire.

But if we apply our rule we shall see at once why it is that the diamond is so expensive. Diamonds are very scarce; they are only found in a few parts of the world,

[11] The "Regent," or "Pitt" Diamond, was bought for this sum by the Duke of Orleans.

[12] There is, however, an exception to this rule, for owing to their great hardness, diamonds are used for cutting glass and other very hard substances. Diamonds are also used for cutting and polishing other diamonds, hence the phrase "Diamond cut diamond," to express a conflict between two persons who both possess great strength, cleverness, or power.

chiefly in South Africa and Brazil, and the supply of them therefore is very small.

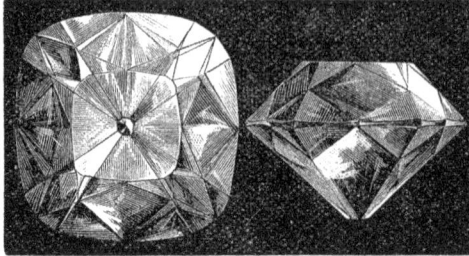

THE REGENT DIAMOND

On the other hand, a very great number of people like to wear so beautiful and rare a stone as the diamond, and such people are to be found, not in one country only, but all over the world. The demand, therefore, for diamonds is very large. Now, according to our rule, where the supply is small and the demand is large, the price will be high, and this case of the diamonds is an example of the correctness of the rule.

Red Herrings

Let us pass from something that is very expensive to something that is very cheap. A red herring, you know, costs very little, generally about ½d. The number of people who eat red herrings is very large indeed. Many millions of herrings are sent from Scotland to London every year, so it is plain there is a very large demand for them, and yet they remain very cheap.

Does this agree with our rule? According to our rule, prices will be high where the demand is great and the supply small. Here the demand is great, and the price is very low. That is quite true, but the supply is not small. On the contrary, the supply of herrings is simply enormous—greater even than the demand. Here is an account of the herring fishery, which will give you some idea of the number of herrings which exist in the seas round the coast of Europe.

The Herring and its Enemies

"The annual take of herrings is prodigious. About a million of barrels, representing 800,000,000 fish, are taken in Scotland. The Norwegian herring fishery is as productive as the Scotch fishery, and the English, the Irish, the French, and the Dutch fisheries are also very productive. Estimating the gross produce of the four fisheries at only the same amount as the Scotch fishery, 2,400,000,000 herrings must be annually taken by these four nations—the British, the French, the Dutch, and the Norwegian.

"Yet the destruction of herring by man is probably insignificant compared with that wrought by other, natural agencies. Cod and ling, of which three and a half million were taken in Scotland in one year, feed largely on herring, six or seven being often found in the stomach of a cod. These, it is thought, consume twelve times as many herring as the four nations together. Gannet, of which 10,000 dwell on Ailsa Craig, must catch more herring than all the fishermen of Scotland.

"Whales, porpoises, seals, cod-fish, dog-fish, predaceous[13] fish of every description are constantly feeding on them from the moment of their birth. The shoals of herring in the ocean are always accompanied

[13] Predaceous = fish that prey on others.

by flocks of gulls and other sea-birds, which are continually preying upon them, and it seems therefore no exaggeration to conclude that man does not destroy one herring for every fifty destroyed by other enemies.

"The destructive power of man therefore is insignificant when it is compared with the destructive agencies which Nature has created, and nothing that man has done, or is likely to do, has produced, or will probably produce, any appreciable effect on the number of herring in the open seas."

A Wonderful "Supply"

You will see from this wonderful account how true the old saying is that "there are more fish in the sea than ever came out of it," and you may also learn from

it the lesson I wished to teach, namely, that in the case of the herrings, which are bought and sold for such small prices, the law of supply and demand holds good.

For while, on the one hand, a great demand and a small supply bring high prices, as in the case of the diamond, so, where the supply is greater than the demand, the price will be low, as in the case of the herrings, of which the supply is so great that it cannot be exhausted.

XVII

More Facts about Tea

And now let us go back to the question which I put at the beginning of this chapter. What is the price of a pound of tea? You remember that we said that a pound of tea might vary very much—from 1s. 6d. up to 10s., and I also said that the price, whether it were ls. 6d. or 10s., was fixed in accordance with rules and reasons; and so it is. The rules which fix the price of a pound of tea are those which we have been speaking about in this chapter.

Tea which costs 10s. a pound is generally some very rare kind of tea, of which but little is grown, and which has some very delicate or peculiar flavour. A great many people are anxious to buy it on account of its rarity and its quality; therefore, in accordance with our rule, the price of it is very high, for the supply is small and the demand is large.

A very great proportion of the tea that is grown in China and India is, however, of a commoner kind. This is the tea which is commonly drunk in England, and, as you know, there are millions of people in England who drink tea every day of their lives.

In order to meet their wants, the tea-planters in China and India cultivate every year a very great number of tea plants, sufficient to supply this country with no less than 182,000,000 pounds weight of tea during the year. Here we have a case in which the demand is very great, but the supply is great also, and the result is that the price is neither very high nor very low, and the tea is usually sold at from 1s. 6d. to 3s. a pound.

Lastly, there is a kind of tea which consists of sweepings and refuse. Of course, as this is only what is left over from the tea which is intended to be sold at a higher price, the quantity must be small as compared with the 182,000,000 pounds which come over to this country. The supply, therefore, is small, but comparatively few people care for this kind of tea when they can get better kinds, and so, though the supply is small, the demand is small too, and the price, instead of going up because of the smallness of the supply, goes down because the demand is also very small, and tea of this kind sells very often for less than 1s. a pound.

Our Question Answered

Thus you will see that it is possible to give a reason for the different prices at which a pound of tea is sold. It is most important that you should understand the meaning of the law of supply and demand, for it explains a great many matters which concern us all very much, and about which we may make great mistakes if we are not very careful to understand their true reasons.

SUMMARY

THE LAW OF SUPPLY AND DEMAND

1. The Laws of Nature and Reason are to be learnt from observation and experience.

2. Our daily life is governed by these laws: it is therefore most important to learn and to obey them.

3. Such common things as buying and selling, working and wage-earning, spending and saving, are governed by these laws.

4. One of the most important of these laws is that of "supply and demand."

5. The price of any article is regulated by the law of supply and demand.

6. Where the demand is large and the supply small, the price will be high.

7. Where the demand is small and the supply great, the price will be low.

8. Where both supply and demand are large, the price will generally be low.

CHAPTER VI

CHANGES IN SUPPLY AND DEMAND

XVIII

An Endless Supply

Now that we have got so far towards understanding what is meant by the law of supply and demand, and know that prices depend upon it, we shall be able to go a step further. We have seen that if there be a great demand and a small supply prices will go up, and it is natural to ask next what it is that makes a supply or a demand great or small.

The supply of some things, such as air and daylight, is usually endless. There is generally more air and more daylight in the world than are required to satisfy the demand of every man, woman, and child in the world. It is only on very rare occasions that the supply of air or daylight is greatly interfered with, and man's industry does nothing to supply them.

A Supply which Depends on Work

There are other things, such as corn, of which the supply is very great, but the quantity of which, nevertheless, depends upon the work of men; for though, of course, it is true that the grains of wheat grow and ripen in the course of Nature, yet without men to plant and cultivate the grain, to plough, to reap, to gather, to thresh, to winnow, and to grind, the supply of corn, which is now so great, would cease. Thus you see corn is one of those things the supply of which depends upon the hard work and skill of those who are employed in cultivating it.

The Supply of Gold

Then there are such things as gold and precious stones, which are found in a few places, and which are to be got only with great difficulty. The supply of these will depend, for the most part, on accident and chance, and comparatively little upon the efforts of men.

For instance, the supply of gold was very much increased by the discovery of gold in Australia in 1851, and since the discovery the efforts and skill of the miners have helped to bring to the surface of the ground a large quantity of the precious metal. But, however anxious men may be to work, however much they may wish for gold, however skilful they may be in searching for it, they cannot increase the supply of gold in the same way as they can increase the supply of corn; and even now the amount of gold raised in Australia is diminishing, and is less than it was when the gold-fields were first discovered.

It is well to remember all these things about the laws of supply, and to understand the division between those things of which there is an endless natural supply dependent upon the work and skill of men, and those of which the supply depends to some extent on the efforts of men, but to a much greater extent upon causes beyond human control.

The Causes of a Demand

What, then, are the causes upon which demand depends, and which make men anxious to possess things? You will find that there are a great many causes. In the first place, with regard to those things which are necessary to life, such as food and drink, everybody must eat in order to live, so there will always be a great demand for some kind of provisions.

Things in General Demand

Then again, except among the most savage races, there will always be a demand for clothes. They are necessaries of life among all civilised people. Then there are other things which in some parts of the world would not be considered necessaries at all, but which we in this country could scarcely do without, such things for instance as tables and chairs, books and newspapers, carriages and carts. For such things as these, the demand increases according as the world becomes more civilised, and the wants of people more numerous.

Luxuries

Lastly, there are those things which we are accustomed to call luxuries, which are not actually necessary in order to keep people from starving, to protect them from wind and weather, or to enable them to carry on their business. Beautiful pictures, statues, flower gardens, pianos, and many other things come under the head of luxuries. But, as you know, though these things are not absolutely necessary, many people are most anxious to possess them.

SOME LUXURIES

Changes in Demand

I have now told you about some of the different classes of things of which there is a supply, and for which there is a demand. A great number of circumstances may happen to make the supply of any article increase or diminish, and in the same way many causes may bring about a change in the demand. We saw that when the supply of any article alters the price of it alters too, and so also when the demand alters the price rises or falls.

XIX

The Cotton Famine

For instance, during the terrible war that took place in the United States of America, between 1860 and 1864, there was a very great scarcity of cotton in Lancashire. At the time I speak of, nearly the whole of the cotton used for manufactures in this country came from the Southern part of the United States, and most of it on arrival was taken to the mills in Lancashire to be woven into calico.

As the war went on however, the Northern States began to blockade or shut up the Southern harbours from which the cotton came. New Orleans, the great city at the mouth of the Mississippi, was closely watched by the Northern ships of war, and no vessels were allowed to go in or out. It was hoped by this means to compel the South to give in, and thus to bring the war to an end.

It was not however the people of the South only who suffered from the blockade. The cotton which was required for the Lancashire mills never arrived, and most of the mills had to be shut up. Not only was the very greatest distress inflicted on the workpeople, who were thus turned out of work by no fault of their own, but the supply of calico and cotton goods of every kind fell short, owing to the impossibility of obtaining cotton.

Lancashire's Misfortune— Yorkshire's Opportunity

Now from this scarcity of cotton arose a very remarkable result, but one which, if you think a little, was natural enough. Next to the great county of Lancashire lies the still greater county of Yorkshire. In Lancashire the great industry upon which most people are engaged, is, as I told you, the making of cotton goods. In Yorkshire the manufacture of cotton is replaced by the manufacture of woollen goods, such as alpacas, mohairs, broadcloths, serges.

A SPINNING FRAME

It is hard to come to an end of the materials of which dresses are made nowadays, but with the exception of such costly things as silk dresses, nearly all gowns are made of either wool or cotton in some shape or another.

Tastes vary; some people prefer an alpaca to a print, some like a cotton gown better than a serge. And the wearing of cotton or wool of course depends not only upon the taste of the wearer, but upon other things, such as the time of year and the cost of the material. So when there is no more difficulty in getting one than the other, all that buyers need do is to make up their minds which they prefer.

So too with such things as shirts; some people prefer flannel shirts, others prefer cotton shirts, and the cotton ones have the advantage of cheapness. But at the time of the American war the usual condition of things soon became altered. Cotton was very scarce, and in consequence all goods made of cotton soon became very dear and difficult to get. But the supply of wool was not interfered with by the fighting in America.

Hence, you can easily see that the woollen manufacturers soon found that there was an advantage on their side. The choice between cotton and wool no longer depended upon taste or fancy, nor even upon the time of year. Many of those who usually bought cotton goods and preferred to do so, were unable to pay the high prices which were now charged for cotton, and they were therefore compelled to spend in alpacas, serges, mohairs, and flannel, what they had formerly spent in calicoes and other Manchester goods.

Wool for Cotton

The Yorkshire manufacturers were not slow to take advantage of their good fortune. The demand for their goods kept increasing even faster than they could supply it, and soon every mill in Yorkshire was as busy as it could be. The price of woollen goods went up, for the demand was for a time even greater than the supply; and so matters continued very prosperously for the Yorkshire mills, and very unfortunately for the Lancashire mills, until the end of the war.

Then once more matters returned to their natural state. Cotton could again be bought cheap and in large quantities. Lancashire was once more able to offer its goods at the old prices, and soon the Yorkshire manufacturers found that they must again bring down their prices to the old figure, lest all their customers should desert them and take to the cheap Manchester goods. Thus you will see how prices rise and fall with a change in the demand.

XX

Freaks of Fashion

Sometimes very strange results are brought about by changes in fashion, which make more difference to the question of demand than we should at first think possible. Fashions may spring up that will create a demand for the strangest things, which had little or no value before the fashion sprang up, and which cease to have any as soon as the fashion has changed.

The Queen of Flowers

Here is an instance of what I mean. All flowers are beautiful objects in themselves, and a source of pleasure to those who love the works of Nature. A rose, a violet, a tulip, a lily are all valued on account of their colour,

THE ROSE, THE LILY, THE VIOLET, AND THE TULIP

their fragrance, their shape, or the brightness of their hues. The rose has been called the "Queen of Flowers," and in all ages it has been a favourite of flower-lovers. The little violet has been the chosen flower of many; nor has the lily, with its pure white bells, been without its champions who would put it first among all the flowers.

The tulip, too, is a handsome flower, with its bright open cup and its great variety of tints. It has not, however, the fragrance of the rose or the violet, nor has it the grace and the exquisite shape of the lily. It is impossible not to admire the tulip, but no one would have expected that it should have been at one time the costliest and the most sought after of all the flowers that grow. Yet, thanks to a strange freak of fashion, such was actually the case.

An Odd Demand

In the seventeenth century there arose in Holland an extraordinary fancy for growing tulips. Hundreds and thousands of pounds were spent by rich people in buying the bulbs of these flowers. Whenever a new kind of tulip was discovered there were many buyers anxious to purchase it. Some kinds were very rare, and, above all, a black tulip had never been known.

An untold amount of money and care were expended in efforts to obtain a black tulip. The bulbs of the various flowers were sold according to their weight and rarity. For one root a purchaser agreed to give 4,600 florins, together with a new carriage, two grey horses, and a complete harness; while another was bought for twelve acres of land.

Such was the effect of a freak of fashion in creating a demand for a thing which in itself was of little value and no use. I have told you the story to show you that cases will sometimes arise in which things as useless as the Dutch tulips may suddenly rise into favour, become *fashionable,* and be in great demand.

When this happens, the price will, of course, remain high just as long as the fashion lasts; and no longer. Now and then in this country a cruel fashion springs up of using the wings and feathers of birds to decorate women's hats and dresses. Then of course the value of the poor gulls and goldfinches and other birds, which are killed to supply these ornaments, goes up in consequence of the fashion.

In talking of supply and demand, we must not forget the effect of fashion in raising a demand.

XXI

A Demand that Passes Away

Again, it may happen that some mistaken idea may give rise to a demand, which will continue until it is discovered that the idea is wrong and has no truth in it. Let me give you an odd example of this. Nobody would think that there could be much demand for vipers; indeed, we should imagine that the only thing that such poisonous creatures could be sought out for would be to kill them and get rid of them. But you will see that this has not always been the general opinion.

For many centuries vipers, or some parts of

their bodies, were believed by some physicians to be a valuable medicine and, even as late as the reign of Queen Anne, they were regularly used by well-known doctors. Here is an advertisement taken from one of the papers of that time:—

> *"Whereas the viper hath been a medicine approved by the physicians of all nations, there is now prepared the volatile spirit[14] compound of it, a preparation altogether new, not only exceeding all volatiles and cordials whatsoever, but all the preparations of the viper itself. It is the most sovereign remedy against all fainting, sweating, lowness of spirits, vapours, &c."*

Here you will see that a demand existed for an article which you and I and most people nowadays would certainly be only too glad to go without; and, as a matter of fact, the demand, as usual, led to a supply, and vipers were regularly caught and sold to those who believed, or tried to make others believe, in this strange method of using them.

Difference of Supply in Two Places

It is important to remember that what is very cheap in one place may be very dear in another. You can think of many examples of the truth of this fact, but you will find that in all cases the difference in price is to be explained by the same laws of supply and demand which we have been talking about.

Nothing that man can do will make any difference to the great waters of the ocean. Anyone at the seaside

[14] Volatile spirit $=$ a spirit which easily evaporates, or turns to vapour.

would be at liberty to take as much water as he chose out of the sea, and do what he liked with it.

Certainly he would make no difference to the sea, and certainly also no one would give him a farthing for the salt water which he had got when there were millions and millions of tons of it to be had for nothing. But though salt water at the seaside is of no value at all, there are many places in which it is of great value, and in which considerable prices are paid for it.

A LARGE SUPPLY

Ice Cliffs near *the North Pole*

The Price of a Gallon of Sea-water

Those of you who know London may have seen carts carrying cans of sea-water from the railway stations to private houses. There are many people who are willing to pay 6d. for a can of sea-water for a bath; and thus you will see that the very same thing which in one place costs nothing, costs a good round sum in another.

Why is this? It is because at the seaside the supply is far greater than the demand, while in London the demand can only be met by those who have undertaken the trouble and expense of getting the water out of the sea, bringing it by train for 60 or 70 miles, and distributing it at the houses of those who require it. The supply, therefore, is small and, what before had no price, is now bought and sold. And so it is with a hundred other articles which you can think of.

Mineral Waters and Penny Ices

Near the banks of the River Rhine, in Germany, there gushes from the ground a bright and clear stream of water. If no one but those in the neighbourhood drank the water of this stream, it would be worth little more than any common brook; but this water has some special qualities. It is sparkling, pleasant to the taste, and good for the health. Very large quantities of it, therefore, are put into bottles every year and sent to England and to all parts of the world, and by the time it is placed upon the table of a Londoner or a Parisian, each pint of water has come to cost 2d. or 3d.

The ice which forms the great glaciers of Switzerland,

or which covers the broad lakes of Canada, is not only without value in the place where it is formed, but is often a source of danger and loss to man; but cut up into blocks and carried away to warmer countries it becomes of the greatest possible value for many purposes: for the hospital, for the preservation of fruit and vegetables, for the dinner-table, and for making the penny ices and cooling drinks which are sold in the streets.

From these examples you will see how the value of a thing may alter according to the place in which it is, and how this alteration really takes place in obedience to the law of supply and demand.

SUMMARY

CHANGES IN SUPPLY AND DEMAND

1. A *supply* may be—

   a. Endless, as in the case of air and daylight.

   b. It may depend upon man's industry.

   c. It may depend partly upon chance and partly upon man's industry and skill.

2. A *demand* may be—

   a. *General,* as in the case of the demand for food.

   b. *Particular,* as in the case of the demand for books and pictures.

3. A *demand* may vary according to place and time.

4. A *demand* for one article may be increased by the failure in the supply of another. In the American War, the failure in the *supply* of cotton increased the *demand* for wool.

5. A *demand* may be created by a change in fashion.

6. An article of which there is a large supply in one place, and which has little value, may be of great value in another place where the supply of it is small.

The cost of carrying an article from the place where it is found to the place where it is used, must be added to its value.

CHAPTER VII

PRICES

XXII

Going to Market

IN the last chapter we spoke of the law of supply and demand, and I explained to you how it was that the prices of things which are bought and sold are fixed by this law; but you all know quite well that prices are constantly changing. Anybody who has ever gone marketing knows the truth of this. One day you will see Cheshire cheeses selling at 7d. a pound, turkeys at 10d. a pound, eggs at ls. 6d. a dozen, and cabbages at ld. each.

A month later you may go to the same market and find that the cheese is selling at 8d. a pound, the price of turkeys has gone down from 10d. to 8d., that eggs have fallen from ls. 6d, to 1s. per dozen, while cabbages have risen from ld. to 1½d. Here are a number of prices, all fixed by the law of supply and demand, and yet all of them changing from month to month.

How is this? Does it mean that the laws of supply and demand change, or that they are right in one case

MARKET-DAY IN THE COUNTRY

and wrong in another? I need hardly tell you that this is not the case. On the contrary, it is in obedience to the law of supply and demand that the prices change in the way we have seen.

"Poultry Cheap To-day"

Take the case of the turkeys for instance. You may be quite sure that there is very good reason for the price having gone down, and you will find, if you inquire, that one of two things has happened—either there are more turkeys for sale on the second occasion than on the first, that is to say, that the supply has increased, or else fewer people want turkeys, or in other words, that the demand has diminished. Or, indeed, it may happen that there are more turkeys in the market and fewer people who want to buy them; in other words, that the supply has increased and the demand has diminished at the same time.

When this happens prices will go down very quickly indeed. What is true of the prices of the turkeys, the eggs, and the cabbages, is true also with regard to the prices of all other things that are bought and sold. The price will vary from time to time according to the supply and demand.

XXIII

The Law of Prices

I have spoken to you only of things which are bought and sold in very small quantities at a time, and for very small prices, but the same thing is equally true about those things which are sold in very large quantities, and for which the price is often many thousand pounds.

The Price of Bread

The corn which we grind into flour to make bread costs a very great sum. The value of the wheat brought into this country during a single year is sometimes as much as £24,000,000, but the price paid for the wheat changes greatly from time to time. Sometimes it is 30s. a quarter, sometimes 35s., sometimes even as much as 40s. a quarter. Whatever may be the price, you may be sure that there is a reason for it. In 1880 no less than forty-one and a half million hundredweight of wheat were brought into this country from America, but in 1886 the quantity brought was only nineteen and a half millions, twenty-two millions less.

AN ARTICLE IN GREAT DEMAND

There are many things which may bring about such a difference as this. If, for instance, there is a bad harvest in America, much less corn will be brought over to this country, for the Americans themselves will be able to spare less of all that is grown in their country, and less will, of course, be brought over to England.

Everybody in England must eat bread, and whether the harvest in America be good or bad we shall want the corn just the same; that is to say, the demand will remain the same. But if less corn comes over to this country the supply will, of course, be less, and, by the law of supply and demand, the price will increase, and corn will become dear.

How High Prices affect Supply

There is one very remarkable result of the law of supply and demand which I ought not to pass over. It very often happens that the effect of high prices is to increase the supply of an article, and sometimes the increase is so great that instead of the demand being greater than the supply, the supply soon becomes greater than the demand, and when this happens the price, of course, according to our rules, will fall.

It is not hard to see how this comes about. Everybody likes to get a high price for what he has got to sell, and directly it becomes known that in any particular place a high price is being paid for a certain article, every one who is the possessor of such an article will do his best to bring it to the place where it is wanted, in the hope of obtaining a high price for it.

Those who come first will certainly make a profit, but the good luck will not last long, for the more people bring their goods to the market the greater will be the supply, till at last the supply becomes greater than the demand, and instead of every seller getting a high price, some will not be able to sell at all.

GIBRALTAR

XXIV

The Siege of Gibraltar

In 1779, when the English were being besieged at Gibraltar by the Spaniards and French, it became very difficult to obtain any provisions, and, on more than one occasion, the garrisons were nearly starving.

The Spanish ships lay close to the fortress and endeavoured to prevent any ships bringing relief to the besieged, and the crews of all the vessels which they took were sent as prisoners into the Spanish gaols. When it became known that the garrison of Gibraltar were in such distress, many persons fitted out ships to carry provisions and other necessaries to them. They were willing to run the risk of being taken by the Spaniards, because they knew that if they were lucky enough to escape they were certain of getting a very high price for their cargoes.

Famine Prices

Nor were they mistaken. Here is a list of the prices of some of the articles sold during the siege:—

	£	s.	d.
Fresh Beef per lb.	0	4	10½
Pork ,,	0	4	1
Fowls per couple	1	1	11½
A Goose	1	10	4
A Turkey	2	8	9
Cheese per lb.	0	4	1
Salt Butter ,,	0	4	1
Eggs per doz.	0	4	0
Potatoes per lb.	0	2	6
Loaf Sugar ,.	0	17	1
Tea ,,	2	5	6
Flour	0	2	1
Candles	0	2	6

How would you like to have made a pudding, with butter at 4s. per lb., eggs at 4d. each, sugar at 17s. per lb., flour at 2s. a lb., and milk not to be obtained at any price?

Supply and Demand Again

Thus you see that the needs of the garrison induced many people to undertake a risk and a danger which, under ordinary circumstances, they would never have cared to run. The demand created the supply, and as long as the demand remained greater than the supply the high prices were kept up.

Gibraltar Saved—Well done, General Elliot!

At last, however, after our gallant troops had been besieged for three years and five months, they were rewarded by a well-earned victory. A great bombardment of Gibraltar was undertaken by the French and Spanish forces, and from sea and land thousands of shot and shell were showered upon the defenders; but General Elliot, who was in command of the garrison, was not daunted by so fierce an attack.

He gave orders that the cannon should be loaded with red-hot shot and pointed at the ships. Soon the enemy's vessels began, one by one, to burst into flames, and by nightfall their whole fleet was either destroyed or thrown into the utmost confusion.

There was no longer any hope left of taking Gibraltar, and a few weeks later a peace was signed, which left the great fortress in the hands of England.

How the Prices Fell

But I must not forget that I am only telling you about the siege of Gibraltar in order to furnish an example of the rules of supply and demand. No sooner was it known that the siege was at an end than from all quarters vessels came in laden with provisions and stores of every kind.

Where there had been want and famine there was now abundance, and ere long, not only had the high prices of the siege-time passed away, but, owing to the vast number of sellers who had been persuaded to bring their wares to such a rich market, far more was brought than was actually wanted, and prices fell to a lower rate than they had ever been at, even before the siege began.

XXV

Supply Created by Demand

You will easily see that there is another result which may be brought about by the existence of a great demand and a small supply. In the case I have just told you about the demand did not create the means for supplying it. The ships and the provisions were all in existence while the siege was going on; they were only brought together at Gibraltar by the great demand which there was for them. But sometimes not only will the demand bring to a certain place articles which are to be found elsewhere, but it will lead to the production of articles which did not previously exist.

Dear Bread

Let me give you an example of this. During the great war between England and France, which lasted almost without a break from 1793 to 1815, the supply of corn in England fell short of what was required by the inhabitants.

There were two causes for this scarcity. In the first place, it was difficult and dangerous to bring corn over the sea at a time when every ship ran the chance of being captured by an enemy; and in the second place, even if corn were successfully brought to England, it could only be sold at a very high price because of the taxes which were put upon it by Parliament.

The expenses of carrying on the war were very great, and those who then directed the government of the country thought it wise to collect the money necessary for the army and navy by taxing the corn. This was not, indeed, a wise manner of getting the money, and nowadays we have altogether given up the plan of taxing the bread of the people; but at the time I am speaking of, the plan found general approval.

In the first place, it was a very easy way of collecting the money; and in the second place, it gave a great advantage to all those who were the owners of land in this country. Everyone was obliged then, as they are now, to buy corn, or rather to buy bread, and by keeping out corn from abroad the owners of the land were able to compel all those who wanted bread to come to them to purchase it.

A Demand, and How it was Met

The land of England on which wheat was grown soon proved insufficient to supply the needs of all the people of England; in other words, the supply was not equal to the demand. Two results sprang from this fact. To begin with, there was great distress throughout the country owing to the scarcity and dearness of bread. There was also another result, which, if you have attended to what I have told you in this chapter, you will easily guess.

The demand being very great and the supply small, prices rose, and as soon as prices became high a great many people came forward anxious to sell their wheat in a market where such good profits were to be made; but there is an old proverb which says that "You cannot have more of a cat than its skin," and so also you cannot have more than one crop of wheat in a year off a field.

There were a certain number of fields in England upon which wheat was sown, and though by very careful farming rather more might be got from them than heretofore, still it was impossible to add very much to their produce.

But another way out of the difficulty was discovered. There was a great deal of land in England which, up to that time, had not been considered good enough to grow wheat upon. It was either land of a poor quality, requiring much expensive manure to enable it to produce a good crop, or else it was land situated on mountain sides, far from a road, or in some place which it was difficult to get to.

So long as the price of wheat was low nobody cared to cultivate such land, for the expense of doing so would have been greater than the profit which would have been made. As soon, however, as the war and the taxes upon foreign corn began to diminish the supply of wheat, the prices paid for it in England began to go up.

PLOUGHING UP THE PASTURES

The farmers and owners of land soon found this out, and took advantage of it. They set to work to plough up land on the hill-sides which had never before been cultivated, and to make roads to distant spots where the ploughshare had never gone before. In these new fields they grew wheat, and though it is true that at the old price they would have been the losers by doing so, the high prices now enabled them, not only to bear the extra expense of cultivating the bad land, but allowed them to get a good profit for their corn after all expenses were paid.

Thus, you see, the increased demand led to an increased supply, for by raising the price of corn it made more people anxious to grow and to sell it.

The Bread Taxes

Nor have we come to the end of the lesson which may be learnt from this example. In 1815 the great war between England and France came to an end, and the danger to ships upon the sea came to an end. Here was one cause which helped to make wheat expensive taken away. Vessels bringing wheat into this country were no longer in danger of being captured by an enemy; but the danger from French ships had very much less to do with the high price of wheat than had the laws of which I have already spoken, by which a tax was put upon all wheat coming into the United Kingdom from over the sea.

It made very little difference to the owner of a cargo of wheat that his ship arrived safely at Liverpool, if when he came to sell the wheat he found himself obliged to pay a tax upon every bushel, which took away all his profit and left him poorer instead of richer for his pains.

While the tax upon corn was kept up, the price of wheat therefore remained very high, and farmers continued to cultivate land which at one time had lain idle.

The "Repeal of the Corn Laws"

At last, however, in the year 1846, a great change came. The Corn Laws were repealed, and the taxes upon wheat done away with altogether. Immediately from all parts of the world where wheat could be grown cheaply large supplies began to come in.

Cheap Corn, and the Effects of it

The price fell, for the supply had become greater. Gradually it became impossible to grow wheat profitably upon the new land which had been cultivated during the existence of the tax. English farmers were no longer able to fix the price at which corn should be sold, for if they did not sell cheap, those who brought the corn from America, from India, from Egypt, and from Australia did, and they found themselves obliged either to lower their prices or to keep their wheat unsold.

Soon, therefore, the new fields began to be abandoned, and year by year the land which, during the time of high prices, had come under the plough, now went back into fields of grass, such as it had been to start with. In many parts of England now uncultivated, you can see the marks of the old enclosures which surrounded the corn-fields, and the marks of the furrows still on the surface.

In Wiltshire, for instance, all over the chalk downs which form the great plain known as Salisbury Plain, these marks of enclosure may be seen everywhere, reminding us that not very long ago there was not a corner of the downs which was not covered with wheat-fields at a time when high prices made it profitable for the farmers to cultivate such land.

Thus from the history of wheat-growing in our country we may learn some useful lessons. We learn, in the first place, how a great demand and a small supply will make high prices. When all the country wanted bread, and only the farmers of the United Kingdom were allowed to supply them, the price of a 4 lb. loaf was as much as ls. 4d., or even ls. 8d.

In the second place, we see how high prices increase the means of supply, for it was the high prices that led the farmers to plough up Salisbury Plain and to grow wheat there. And, lastly, we see how, when the supply is allowed to become very great, prices will go down, for at present, when the supply of wheat comes to us freely from all parts of the world, the price of the 4 lb. loaf has gone down from ls. 4d. to 6d., and the price of a quarter of wheat from 110 shillings to 30 shillings.

SUMMARY

PRICES

1. Prices are fixed by the law of supply and demand.

2. Where the demand is great and the supply small the price will be high.

3. Where the demand is small and the supply large the price will be low.

4. A great demand will often help to create a supply.

5. Every new supply will help to bring down the price of an article for which there is a great demand.

CHAPTER VIII

WORK AND WAGES

XXVI

The Rate and Value of Wages are fixed by Rule

By far the greater number of men and women have to work for their living. They are paid in many different ways, and, as you know, the wages received for the work vary very much. But in some very important matters all kinds of work and all rates of wages are governed by the same laws—laws which never change, and which can be understood by those who choose to study them with attention.

It would seem at first as if there could be no rule, but that in every fresh case where a man or woman undertook to do a piece of work a fresh bargain must be made between the worker and the employer.

And, indeed, it is true that every man or woman who works for wages, of whatever kind, does really make such a bargain before he or she begins to work. It is true that there are many thousands of such agreements made, each differing both as regards the sum to be paid, the work to be done, and the length of time to be occupied in doing the work.

A labourer may be employed for a day to dig a ditch, and may receive 2s. as wages. A girl may go into service for a month, and receive £2. A soldier may engage to serve for seven years at 1s. a day. And of course many other instances could be given, so unlike one another that it would seem quite impossible that any general rule or rules could apply to them all.

A LABOURER'S WORK

We must Learn the Rules

And yet there is no doubt at all that there are such rules, which we may discover if we choose, and which will go on working in spite of us if we fail to pay attention to them.

As I told you, men always suffer in the end if they

try to work against the great rules of nature and reason, and so it is well worth while, in this as in other cases, to try and find out what are the rules and laws which govern the payment of wages, and which we are bound to obey in the long run, whether we like it or not.

DRIVER AND STOKER ON THE FOOT-PLATE
OF THE EXPRESS ENGINE

Workers and their Wage

You know that in every trade there are different rates of wages for different kinds of work, and that very often two men are paid different rates for the same kind of work. You can think of hundreds of examples of this if you take a little trouble.

For instance, a bricklayer is paid more than a carter, although the latter may work just as many hours as the former; and an engine-driver is paid more than a stoker, although both driver and stoker spend their day together on the footboard of the same engine; and, lastly, you know it often happens that of two workmen employed on the same job—say, as cutters in a tailor's shop, or as mechanics in a factory—one will receive more wages than the other.

What are the Rules?

What is it that settles how these workers are to be paid? Why is it that one receives more than another? Can we find out who will get the highest wages? Let us turn to our laws and rules, and see if they will help us.

In the first place, in order that work should be paid for at all, there must be a *demand* for it—that is to say, there must be somebody who wants it done, and who is willing to pay for it. Secondly, work for which there is a demand, but which only few people are able to do, will be paid for at a higher rate than work which can be done equally well by a great number of people.

It is always easiest to understand rules by the help of examples, so I will give you some examples, showing the truth of these rules. Meanwhile you must not forget what it is we are trying to find out in this chapter. We are trying to find out what are the great rules which govern the rate of wages, and which determine who shall receive high, and who shall receive low, wages.

XXVII

There must be a Demand

Rule 1, put shortly, is this: *"Wages will only be paid when there is a demand for the work done by the wage-earners."*

Dean Swift, who wrote "Gulliver's Travels," tells us of a strange country inhabited by very odd people, who were busily engaged on work of a truly extraordinary kind. Some of the busiest were at work upon a plan for extracting sunbeams from cucumbers, while others were softening marble for pillows and pincushions.

The people of Lagado (that was the name of the strange town) were only an invention of Swift's brain, but they are meant to furnish us with an example of those people who work hard upon tasks which are neither worthy and useful in themselves, nor likely, however long they may be continued, to produce any result which will be of use to mankind.

We can get sunbeams without manufacturing them out of cucumbers, and we can get them at no greater expense than is involved in taking a walk in the sunshine. You may depend upon it, therefore, that even had the machines spoken of in Dean Swift's fairy tale been really invented, there would have been no demand for them. No one, therefore, would have been willing to pay wages to the workmen who were employed in making them, for, as our rule tells us, "wages will only be paid when there is a demand for the work done by the wage-earners."

This is a rule which should be remembered by all who have to decide in what way they will learn to get their living. To work hard and to work well is not always a certain road to earning a living: a worker must consider whether what he is learning to do is something which somebody else wants done. You may be perfectly sure that if it be not wanted the worker will never earn a living by such work.

XXVIII

Another Rule

Rule 2. *Work for which there is a demand, but which only few people are able to do, will be paid for at a higher rate than work which can be done equally well by a great number of people.*

This is a very important rule, and you will see that it helps to explain many of the puzzling questions with respect to work and wages. You will see, if you think for a moment, that the work which only a few people are able to do, must be work which it is either difficult to do, disagreeable to do, or dangerous to do. Almost every one can do easy work, but only a few can do work that is very difficult, and only a few will consent to do work which is very disagreeable or dangerous.

And thus you will find that as a rule the more difficult, the more dangerous, the more disagreeable work is, the higher will be the wages paid to those who do it. It is not because the work is hard or disagreeable that the wages are high, but it is because those who do the work are few. For, as I told you in the rule, work for which there is a demand, but which only a few people can do, will be better paid than work which can be done by a great number of persons.

A Bricklayer and a Carter

Why is a bricklayer paid more than a carter, although he works no longer and no harder? It seems hardly fair at first that one should have such an advantage over the other. But think for a moment, and you will see that it is not only fair, but that it must be so. Which is harder to do—to lead a cart or to set a wall of bricks? It is easy enough to lead a cart that is certain, and perhaps some of you think it is easy enough to lay bricks and to make a wall.

If you do, it only shows that you have not paid much attention to the way houses are built, and to the care that has to be taken in laying and fastening the bricks. No; even the plainest kind of bricklaying has to be done by rule and method, and can only be done properly by those who have learnt their trade. To learn a trade it is necessary to serve an apprenticeship, and in the case of the bricklayer this apprenticeship would last several years, and during all that time the apprentice would receive no wages, or very small wages, and would have to be supported by his parents and friends.

So you see here at once there is a difference between the bricklayer and the carter; the former has to give much more time and attention to learning his trade than the latter.

But everybody has not time enough or money enough to be able to wait several years before he begins to receive wages for his work, and the number of those who can wait, and who can spend money, will generally be less than the number of those who are compelled to set to work upon the first employment in which they can use their hands and their strength, and which will bring them enough wages to enable them to live.

Hence it is that in this country persons who are only able to do work which requires strength without skill or special knowledge, are usually paid less than those who have prepared themselves for their work by education, and have gone through an apprenticeship or a long training before they have started in their trade or profession.

Head-Work and Hand-Work

It is for this reason that persons who work with their heads generally receive a higher reward for their work than those who work with their hands. It may seem at first sight unfair that a doctor who gives advice to a sick person, and who does nothing more than speak a few words and give directions about the proper medicine to be taken, should receive as much as a guinea for his trouble, while a labouring man, who works hard all day loading a wagon or digging a trench, receives for his whole day's work 2s. or 2s. 6d. only.

XXIX

The Cost of Learning

But you must remember that before the doctor learnt his business, before he was allowed to give advice to the sick and to prescribe medicine for his patients, he had to spend five, six, and perhaps even seven years in studying his profession. During that time he was obliged to pay for expensive books and expensive teachers; he had to give up months to attending in the hospitals, and he had to pass difficult examinations, before the law allowed him to do any work at all.

Meanwhile, of course, he had to live, and not only to pay for his food and lodging, but for all the expensive teaching which I have told you of, and all the time for five, six, or seven years he was obliged to be spending money instead of earning it.

When, therefore, at last the time comes that the doctor is able to undertake the work of his profession, and to receive payment for what he does, it will be necessary for him to repay himself the loss which he has undergone during all the previous years of preparation. No one would be willing to go on spending large sums of money in preparation for work year after year without the hope of a time coming at last when he would be able to reap the fruits of his industry and self-sacrifice.

The labourer who loads a cart or digs a trench is paid simply for using his strength for a certain length of time to do a particular piece of work; but when the doctor receives his fee he is paid not only for the time and trouble which he has taken in giving advice at the moment, but for the skill and knowledge which he has used in giving that advice, and for the time and money which he has sacrificed in obtaining his skill and knowledge.

And the same thing is true of all other professions, and the same reasons will explain why it is not always that work which seems the hardest or the most trying which is paid the highest.

A blacksmith will shoe your horse for you, and will charge you a shilling a shoe. A watchmaker will put a new spring in your watch, and it will cost you perhaps five shillings. Here both the blacksmith and the watchmaker must have given care and study to acquire the special knowledge which they possess, but the skill which is required to deal with the delicate works of a watch is greater than that required to forge and hammer a horse-shoe, and so we see the greater skill commands the higher price.

The Makers of the Railway

When a great railway has to be made, two very different kinds of work have to be done. The engineer of the line has to work out all the plans, and to calculate beforehand how every mile of the railway is to be made, where it is to go, and what it is to cost. You will see him at work in his study or in the open air making notes in a little pocket-book, looking through a telescope, examining the country through which the railway is to go, and undergoing very little bodily exertion. But

THE BLACKSMITH'S FORGE

without the engineer's work the railway could not be made.

Soon the actual work of construction will be begun, and then you will see hundreds of fine, strong, muscular men working with all their might digging and filling barrows and wagons, breaking up rocks, building high embankments, and making deep cuttings. These are the railway navvies.[15] No one can doubt whether they are working or not. There are no better and harder workers in the world than the English navvies. Without them and their work the railway could not be made.

Yet when we come to inquire which of the two receives the higher wages, the engineer who plans or the navvies who carry out the work, we shall find that the higher wages go to the former, even though the toil and fatigue which he has to undergo are as nothing compared with what the navvy has to bear.

Skill must be paid for

And now we come back to the same explanation. The skill which the engineer possesses has been acquired only after long years of careful study and at a great cost— he has learnt to do what others cannot do, and therefore he can ask a high price for services which many people require, but which few can give. The navvy, on the other hand, though he works hard and works well, is doing what many thousands of other strong and willing men in the country are able to do.

---

[15] *Navvies.* So called because the first workers on the railways were the "navigators," or makers of the "navigation canals," by which most of the heavy traffic in the country was sent.

The demand for his work is great, but the supply of workers such as he is great also.

Do not suppose, however, that there is anything in head-work, as distinguished from hand-work, which makes it at all times and in all cases the more valuable of the two. The price of work, as I have told you, depends upon the laws of supply and demand, and not upon whether the work be done with the brain or with the hand.

An Unhappy Village

If you can fancy a village to be so unlucky as to possess fifty doctors and only one baker, it is not hard to guess that the baker would have more work to do than any one of the doctors. Nay, more than that, the baker if he chose could get a better price for his loaves than the doctors for their prescriptions. The demand for bread would be very great, and the supply would be small, for there would be only one man to bake for the village.

On the other hand, there would be far more doctors ready to prescribe than patients wishing to take their advice. You may be sure, therefore, that doctors' fees would go down to a very low figure. Nobody, it is true, ever heard of a village which was quite so badly off as the one we have been picturing to ourselves, but many instances are to be found in which a state of things something like that I have described does really exist.

Head-work and Hand-work in the Goldfields

When gold was first discovered in Australia thousands of men flocked over from this country in the hope of making their fortunes by a lucky discovery of the precious metal. The goldfields were in a barren and uncultivated country, where every comfort, and indeed every necessary of life, could be obtained only by hard and difficult work.

The gold-seekers were compelled to build their own huts, to cook their own food, to wash their own clothes, and above all to dig and search for the coveted gold. All these things required bodily strength, and a knowledge of the right way to handle a spade, a pick, a chisel, or a saw. Every man, therefore, who possessed bodily strength and knew how to use his hands, was welcome at the goldfields. But among those who went out were many who at home had been lawyers, clerks, newspaper writers, or who had belonged to other professions in which they had learnt to use not their hands but their heads, whose tool was a pen and not a pick-axe.

For such men as these there was no demand, as they very soon found out to their cost. Nobody would employ them, for they did not know how to dig, and no one wanted their services as lawyers or clerks. The roughest labourer who could dig a trench or saw wood was far better off than men who had spent hundreds of pounds in acquiring an education at college.

The end of it was that some of the head-workers set to work to learn a new trade, and became good hand-workers, and then they too were welcome. Those of them, however, who had not strength or perseverance enough to set to work with their hands soon found themselves in the greatest misery, and looked upon by everybody as useless and good-for-nothing people.

This was not because their knowledge and experience were of no value in themselves, but because in the place to which they had gone the supply of workers such as they was greater than the demand. Thus you will see how hand-workers may receive much better pay than head-workers.

SUMMARY
WORK AND WAGES

1. The rate of wages depends chiefly on the law of supply and demand.

2. In order that work should be paid for there must be a demand for it.

3. Work for which there is a demand, but which only a few people are able to do, will be paid for at a higher rate than work which can be done equally well by a great number of people.

4. Head-work is usually paid for at a higher rate than hand-work, because there are generally fewer people who can do the former well.

5. In calculating the value of a man's work it is necessary to take into account the expense and trouble he has been put to in learning how to do it.

6. Hand-work is sometimes more valuable than head-work; the price paid for the former is then higher than that paid for the latter.

CHAPTER IX

THE VALUE OF WAGES

XXX

The Value of Wages

IT is very important to remember that the real value of a man's wages cannot always be judged merely from the sum of money he receives for his work. It would seem at first sight that if a man received 30s. a week in England and 60s. a week for the same work in Canada or Australia, or some other place beyond the sea, that the latter must be just *twice* as well off as the former, for his wages are twice as large.

But though the amount of money received in Canada or Australia may be twice as much as that received in England, it does not follow that it is twice as valuable. For in considering whether wages are high or low, in deciding whether they are what we call good or bad wages, we must take into account not only the amount of pounds, shillings, and pence paid, but their value to the man who gets them.

The value of wages will depend upon what they will buy. What does a man want to buy with his wages? That is the first question we have to ask, and when we know what it is he wants to buy, we can then find out how far the wages he receives will enable him to buy it.

An Englishman when he leaves home and crosses the sea does not change his nature. On the contrary, he generally goes to some other part of our Empire, in which he lives very much in the same way as he lived at home, and where his wants are not very different from what they were in England. Some things you may be quite certain he will want just as much in his new home as he did in his old one. He will want food, drink, lodging and clothes, and all these things, and a good many others, he must pay for out of the wages he receives for his work.

Now suppose when he gets to his new home he finds that the cost of all these things is exactly the same as it was in England, and that at the same time instead of getting 30s. a week as wages he is getting 60s., then, plainly, he will be twice as well off as he was before, and at the end of each week he will have 30s. to spare over and above what he used to earn.

But suppose, on the other hand, he finds that, although his wages are double what they used to be, the cost of everything he has to buy out of his wages is doubled too, then what will be the result? Instead of being better off at the week's end, he will stand exactly where he was: instead of paying 30s. in the week he will have had to pay 60s., and thus he will have gained nothing at all by his higher wages.

It does not, indeed, often happen that a man

finds himself so badly off as this, but it very often does happen that he gains less by high wages than he expected, because he has not taken the trouble to find out beforehand what he will have to pay as well as what he is likely to earn. It is therefore most important that all who go in search of higher wages should learn all they can about the prices of things they will have to buy in the place they are going to. In this way they will learn the *value* as well as the *amount* of the wages.

XXXI

William Wilson thinks about Emigrating

Let me give you an example of what I mean. William Wilson was a workman living in London. He had a wife and two children, and he earned 30s. a week in wages. One day he saw in the papers that in one of the great British colonies workmen were receiving 50s. a week for the same kind of work as that on which he was engaged.

He at once made up his mind that he would leave his old home, cross the sea, and find a new one in a place which held out such bright prospects to him. "Fancy!" said he to his wife, "at the end of every week we shall have 20s. to put by or to spend as we please after all our expenses are paid."

But Wilson was a wise man, and he knew that it was best not to take such a great step as breaking up his home and going across the sea without making quite sure first that there was no mistake in the information he had received.

WILLIAM WILSON CONSULTS HIS WIFE

He takes Advice like a Wise Man

He took counsel with some of his friends, and they talked the matter over thoroughly. "You had best go," said one of them, "to the new Government office, where they will tell you everything you want to know. They call it the Emigrants' Information Office."[16] This was good advice, and William Wilson took it.

[16]Emigrants' Information Office, 31, Broadway, Westminster, S.W.

He went to the office, and he learnt sure enough that 50s. were the wages paid for workmen like himself in the place he was going to. At the office, however, they also gave him a paper which told him some very important things besides the figures about wages. It told him what was the cost of the principal things which he would have to buy with the wages when he received them.

Wilson took the paper, and studied it carefully. At last he made out a sum, which he put down in this way:—

	W. W.'s Wages in his Old Home: £1 10s.	In his New Home: £2 10s.	
		COST OF LIVING.	
		In the Old Home.	In the New.
		Per Week.	Per Week.
		£ s. d.	£ s. d.	
Baker		0 2 1	0 3 2	more
Butcher		0 9 0	0 6 0	less
Butterman, Eggs, &c. ...		0 2 7	0 3 1	more
Grocer		0 1 9	0 2 9	more
Milkman		0 0 6	0 0 6	same
Greengrocer		0 1 3	0 1 3	same
Clothes		0 2 0	0 3 3	more
Rent		0 6 0	0 11 0	more
All other purposes, Books, Travelling, Trade So-ciety, &c.		0 4 10	0 9 0	more
		1 10 0	2 0 0	
			1 10 0	
			0 10 0	more

"Forty from fifty," said Mr. Wilson to himself, "that leaves ten shillings a week, not twenty. I must go and tell Mrs. Wilson that, and perhaps she will change her mind about going."

William Wilson decides to Go

Well, I may tell you that Mr. and Mrs. Wilson did talk it over, and that Mrs. Wilson did not change her mind. She and her husband went out, and soon found themselves prosperous and happy in their new home.

Unlike so many others, they had no disappointment to face. They knew exactly what to expect, because they had been wise enough to find out beforehand. Though they did not at first save 20s. a week, they did put by 10s.; and before long, instead of paying 11s. a week rent for their house, they had bought a house of their own, in which they lived rent free. The lesson they had learnt was to calculate the *value* of wages, and, as you will see, it proved a very useful lesson to them, as it will to you if you understand it thoroughly.

A Question to be Asked

Another thing must always be borne in mind by those who are in search of employment, and who are led to leave their work because they hear of others being better paid than themselves in another place.

You know I told you that the rate of wages depended upon the law of supply and demand; and in accordance with that law, where the demand is great, and the supply small, the price paid will be high. In the case of wages, it often happens that in some newly settled and distant country there will be a great demand for a particular kind of labour, and a very small supply of those who are able to perform it.

Will the Good Wages Last?

At first, therefore, according to the law of supply and demand, the few workers who are on the spot, and who are able to do the work, can ask for and can obtain very high wages for their work. Naturally enough, when others who can do the same work hear of the high wages that are being paid, they are anxious to set off at once to share the good fortune which has fallen to the first comers.

Of course this is quite right, only those who go ought always to remember that the reasons which made wages high in the first instance grow less and less as each new worker goes to supply the demand which has been created. The very fact, therefore, that there is a great demand will be certain before long to bring about a great supply; and, indeed, it often happens that very soon the supply becomes even greater than the demand, and those who hoped to find high wages and plenty of work find either low wages and little work, or sometimes no wages and no work.

It is necessary, therefore, for a man to observe carefully whether a demand has been already supplied or not before he allows himself to be led away in the hope of high wages.

SUMMARY

THE VALUE OF WAGES

1. The value of wages will depend upon what they will buy.

CHAPTER X

CAPITAL

XXXII

A Farmer's Capital

MOST people in this country live chiefly, as you know, upon bread. The bread is made of flour, and the flour from the grains of wheat.

Suppose a farmer possessed six sacks of corn, and ground up the whole of it into flour, and used the flour to make bread for himself and his family. It is true that for a short time he would have enough bread to eat, but his supply would last for a short time only, and when it was all gone he would be in a very bad position, for, as the proverb says, "You cannot eat your cake and have it," and so the farmer, having eaten his corn, could not have it either, but would be left without grain, without flour, and without money to buy either the one or the other.

If farmers were really to behave in this way, their farming would soon come to an end. But, of course, no one does act in so foolish a manner. The farmer takes his six sacks of corn, and, when springtime comes, he ploughs his field, and plants the seed in the furrows he has made.

Then, as the year goes on, the green blades of the young corn appear above the ground and rise higher and higher, and then the ear appears, and at length, as harvest time approaches, the corn swells in the ear, and the green gives place to a ripe gold, and, when the time for reaping comes, the farmer brings back to his farm not six sacks of corn only, but six times six, and, in addition to this, he has a stack of straw, which in itself is of great value to him, either to use in his farmyard or to sell.

Then, supposing that he were to grind up six sacks of grain for his own use, he would have thirty still remaining. Of these he would put aside six to serve as seed for another year, and still there would remain twenty-four sacks, which he might either grind for his own use or sell to others who wanted to buy it.

This is plainly a much better plan than that of turning the first six sacks of corn into flour at once and using them for food. But there is one thing we must not forget.

It is February when the seed is put into the ground; it is August before the corn which springs from it is reaped, and from February to August is seven months, and before the new corn is threshed, and sold, and ground into flour and paid for, is often another five months, and, meanwhile, what is the farmer to do all this time while the seed is lying underground, while the blade is springing, while the ear is ripening, and while the crop is being reaped, threshed, ground, and sold? He cannot go without food all that time, and if he had really nothing but the corn to live upon he would soon starve.

Money and Time are Wanted

Moreover, we must remember that ploughing and sowing, reaping and harvesting, cannot be done in a day, and cannot be done for nothing. Horses and men must be employed to draw and guide the plough; men must be employed to sow, to reap, to thresh, to winnow, and to grind; and, moreover, the plough, the horses, and the various machines required for reaping and threshing, must be paid for; the barns in which the corn is stored, and the sacks in which it is put, must be paid for also; and, lastly, if the farmer has to pay rent for his field, the money for the rent must also be found and paid, while the corn is growing.

How does the Farmer Manage?

How is this difficulty to be settled?—and how is it that the farmer is able to wait a whole season before he receives the fruit of his labour, and the return for the money he has expended? The answer to the question is a simple one. The farmer, before he begins to farm, must possess a certain amount of money which he is prepared to spend upon his farm, and to use for his own wants until the time comes when the result of his work is apparent.

He Must have Capital

If he does not possess such a sum of money, he cannot possibly afford to wait, and if he cannot afford to wait he cannot afford to farm. This sum of money which he must have before he begins to farm is called his *Capital,* and as it is not only in farming, but in nearly all other trades and professions, that capital is required, it is worth while to pay some attention to the word, and to find out exactly what is meant by it, and what are the uses to which capital is put.

What is the Farmer's Capital?

You must not of course suppose that the farmer at the beginning of the year sets about his work with a bag full of money, which he calls his capital, and that as soon as he has paid for his plough and his horses, the wages due to his men, and the rent due for his land, his capital is gone. Not at all: he has only changed its form; and though he has not actually buried the money in the field, he has done what is much better—he has made the field more valuable by the money he has spent upon it.

It is because he has ploughed the field and kept it in good order, and because he has bought machines and tools, and because he has built barns, that his farm is able to produce each year a crop of corn, which he is able to sell for money at the end of the year.

And, again, the six sacks of corn, though they are no longer in the farmer's granary, but buried in the ground, are part of his capital, for by using them he is able to get back, not, it is true, the exact seeds which he sowed, but others to the same amount, *and the additional sacks which the field produces.*

XXXIII

Capital in Other Trades

As I told you, capital is required in nearly every kind of trade and industry, and without capital a great part of the work which is done in the world around us would come to a standstill.

The Ship

A ship can only earn money by her voyages, after she has been completed in every respect, and fitted with proper engines. But it takes from one to three years nowadays to build a large ship, and during that time money must be paid for her construction, and this money is the capital which is invested by the owner of the ship. As in the case of the money spent in ploughing and sowing the field, the money spent upon the ship does not cease to be capital when the ship is built.

On the contrary, the owner has then only changed the form of his capital from the coins—which, if left idle, would bring him no return—into the ship, which will bring him a return for his trouble each time she makes a successful voyage.

Of course, it requires many voyages to repay the whole cost of the ship, and it is not in one year, or two, that the owner gets back the whole value of his money. Suppose the ship costs £60,000 to build, and when she is finished she makes three voyages to India in the year. If the owner is fortunate, he may obtain £4,000 for each

A MERCHANT STEAMER ENTERING PORT

of these voyages, or £12,000 profit in the year. At this rate, it will be five years before he is repaid the money he has spent.

Other Forms of Capital

Let me give you one or two more examples of capital, and the use which is made of it. You have seen in the case of the corn-field and of the ship how capital is required in the cultivation of the land and in the carrying on of a great industry. It is required no less in the building of houses, and in the lending of money, or banking; and, as you will see, it is necessary also in those professions where men work with their brains only, as, for instance, in the profession of a lawyer or of a doctor.

The Builder's Capital

A man who spends his money in building a house puts his capital into it with the hope of getting a return from it. He lets the house to another person, and the person to whom he lets it agrees to pay so much a year for the use of the capital. The sum which is paid in this way is, as you know, called the "rent" of the house.

The Banker's Capital

It is the practice of bankers to lend money to other people who are willing to pay what we call "interest" for the loan of the money. In order that the banker may have money enough to lend, it is necessary that he should have capital before he begins his business.

The Doctor and the Lawyer

But I said that a doctor or a lawyer was obliged to have capital in his business also, and you will soon see that this is so. It is true that when a lawyer sets up business in a town he does not have to spend much money, as a rule, before he begins; but, nevertheless, he has really already got a *capital*, by using which he hopes to get a living.

Before a man is allowed to set up, or, as it is usually called, to "practise," as a lawyer, he is obliged to make himself acquainted with the law: he has to spend money upon teachers and upon books, and he has to pass examinations which require long and careful preparation. Now, while he is thus learning his business he is compelled to spend a large sum of money, and to pass several years without getting any return at all for his trouble and time.

At last he is allowed to "practise": his knowledge of the law, his experience, and the learning which have cost him so much, form the capital with which he carries on his business. The same thing is true of the doctor, who, like the lawyer, has to spend time and money in preparing himself for the very important work of attending the sick. His knowledge and his skill are his capital.

The Mechanic

A good mechanic, who has served his apprenticeship, has his capital also, and he has it in a double form. In the first place, he has, like the lawyer and the doctor, the

128

skill which he has acquired during his apprenticeship; and in the second place, he often has the tools which enable him to carry on his trade and to show his skill.

The Seamstress

A woman who buys a sewing machine uses the machine as her capital for making a livelihood. Nor are these examples of the various forms which capital may take the only ones that can be given. A good character and a good reputation often prove to be a very valuable form of capital, and anything which helps to make a man's property valuable and sought after by others will serve him as capital. It is wonderful how small a thing may sometimes add to the value of a man's capital, and how a mere accident, with which he has nothing to do, and which he would gladly have prevented, gives him a capital which enables him to grow rich.

XXXIV

Some Strange Ways of acquiring Capital

Here is an example which I think will amuse you. The late Mr. Frank Buckland tells a story of a captured tiger, which had been brought to London. "When the ship arrived at the London Docks," so writes Mr. Buckland, "the den was put in a van and placed in Mr. Jamrach's yard in the Ratcliff Highway" (Mr. Jamrach was the buyer of the tiger) "with the bars towards the wall. The den having been thus placed, Mr. Jamrach walked away, when, on turning round a few minutes afterwards, he saw that the tiger had reared herself up on her hind legs, and a board giving way to her pressure, he perceived with horror that she was coming loose out of the den.

"The Tiger that Swallowed the Boy"

"In a few moments the board, which was quite rotten, 'let go,' and out walked the tiger through the yard gate into the street. A little boy, about nine years old, happened to be playing in the street. This little boy, thinking that the tiger was a big dog, walked up to her, and began patting her; the tiger then turned her head, and seized the boy by the shoulder with her tremendous fangs.

"Jamrach immediately running up, grasped the tiger by the loose skin of her neck, but, although a very strong and powerfully built man, he could not hold the beast, who immediately started off down the street at

AN INCREASE IN THE VALUE OF CAPITAL: OR,
"THE TIGER THAT SWALLOWED THE BOY"

a gallop, carrying the boy in her mouth as a cat would a mouse, Jamrach holding on tight all the time to the tiger's neck, and keeping up with long strides by her side, like a groom by the side of a runaway horse.

"Finding that his hold was giving way, he managed to slip the tiger's hind-leg from under her, and she fell to the ground. Jamrach instantly threw his whole weight down on her, and letting go the skin of her neck, fastened his two thumbs behind her ears with a firm grip.

"There tiger, man, and boy lay many minutes altogether in a heap, the man gripping the tiger, the tiger (still holding the boy in her fangs) all the while suffering great pain from the pressure of Jamrach's hands, and from impeded respiration. After a time, one of Jamrach's men was actually bold enough to put his head round the corner to see if he could render his master assistance. Jamrach cried out, 'Bring me a crowbar!'

"The man got a crowbar, and struck the tiger three severe blows on the nose with it, which made her drop the child from her mouth. Jamrach then sent him for some ropes; these ropes, of course, in the confusion, became entangled, and the tiger, watching her opportunity, sprang up, and getting loose, ran back again up the street, Jamrach after her, crowbar in hand; she bolted immediately round the corner, through the yard gate, and leaped into her den from which she had escaped. Once inside, she cowered down, and lay as quiet as possible.

"The child was, strange to say, not much hurt. He had only a bite on the shoulder, which got well in eight days. The poor little fellow, however, was so terribly frightened that he never spoke for four hours."

Now, this tiger was part of the owner's capital, and if it had only been an ordinary animal it would still have been of value to him for the purposes of his show; but you can easily fancy that this particular tiger had acquired a special value from the fact of his having attacked the boy. On the outside of his show the owner wrote up, "Come and see the tiger that swallowed the boy in the Ratcliff Highway."

Most people are very curious, and you may be sure that many more visitors paid their money to see a wild beast which had swallowed a child (though, indeed, in this the owner went rather beyond the truth) than to see an animal which had lived in a quiet and peaceable way all its life.

Thus, you see, an unfortunate accident, for which the owner of the capital—that is to say, of the tiger—was not answerable, and which he would certainly have prevented had he been able, increased the value of his property, and made him certain of a larger profit.

The Weaver of Donchery

Here is another example of the same thing:—

A strange incident took place during the great war between Germany and France, in 1870, which will show you how a man may sometimes acquire a valuable capital without any effort on his own part, and indeed by an occurrence which he would have been glad to prevent.

Napoleon and Bismarck

On the 1st of September, 1870, was fought the terrible battle of Sedan, in which the Germans surrounded and defeated the French troops under the Emperor Napoleon and Marshal MacMahon. On the morning of the 2nd, the Emperor, seeing that all was lost, and that further resistance was impossible, determined to surrender himself and all his army as prisoners to the King of Prussia. Riding out of the town with a few officers, dejected and sorrowful, he sought Count Bismarck, the famous Minister of King William.

The meeting took place at a little village named Donchery, close to Sedan. It was necessary to find shelter and a place to write down the terms of the surrender. By the roadside was a little house inhabited by two brothers, poor men who earned their living as weavers. Into this house the Emperor and Count Bismarck made their way, and there in the weavers' little room they made the agreement by which the Emperor of the French, with 83,000 French soldiers, with their artillery, standards, and everything they possessed, were handed over to the victorious armies of Germany.

Two Results of a Famous Meeting

The meeting which was to make so much difference to all Europe was also to make a great difference to the weavers of Donchery. Soon all the newspapers throughout the world were full of accounts of the celebrated meeting in front of the little cottage; the correspondents described it, and the illustrated papers made pictures of it.

The weavers' cottage had become famous in an hour. The owner was not slow to understand what a stroke of good fortune had befallen him. Many hundreds of houses around Sedan had been ruined and laid waste by the war, his alone had acquired a value which it had never possessed before, and which without the war it would never have earned.

From all parts of the world visitors came to see the spot where the Emperor Napoleon and Count Bismarck had met after the battle of Sedan, and you may be sure that few of the visitors went away without

THE EMPEROR AND COUNT BISMARK
BEFORE THE WEAVERS' HOUSE AT DONCHERY

making some small present to the owner of the house and garden where the famous event took place. Thus it happened that the weaver found himself the owner of a capital which he had done nothing to create, but which, nevertheless, he might look to year by year to give him a steady payment far in excess of the wages he had earned in his trade of weaving.

The house at Donchery still stands as it did on the memorable 2nd of September, 1870, and whether the weaver occupies it or not, you may depend upon it that it is still forming part of the capital of whoever owns it.

XXXV

How to acquire Capital

Now that we have seen what capital is, and how necessary it is in every trade and calling, it is time to inquire how it is that some people manage to obtain more of it than others, and to ask what is its value to those who possess it and to those who do not.

In the first place, how is capital acquired? That is a question to which many answers may be given, for there are so many forms in which capital may exist, that the ways in which it may be acquired are almost endless; but there is one thing which, with a few exceptions, such as those I have given you, is true of every form of capital, and it is this: that *the possession of capital involves saving or sacrifice.*

This does not seem, at first sight, a very easy sentence to understand, but a little explanation will make it clear. If two men are working for wages, each receiving the same amount, the one who saves and puts by money will, in the long run, acquire a capital which his fellow-workman, who spends every week as much as he earns, will never obtain.

Saving and Sacrificing

Suppose, for instance, that a joiner be receiving 30s. a week as wages, and instead of spending the whole sum on his weekly expenses, puts 2s. a week into the savings bank, and pays 1s. as rent for an allotment or small piece of land. Then, again, suppose that during the course of the year he raises fruit and vegetables on his allotment worth £5, he will have transformed the money spent in rent into a capital which brings him an increase of £2 8s. at the end of the year.

And suppose, again, that as soon as he has £5 in the bank he draws it out and spends it in buying better tools than he has before possessed, and is thus enabled to do finer work, for which he receives a large payment, he will then have turned the money which he has saved into capital, in the shape of his tools.

In both cases you must notice that the joiner has sacrificed something and saved something. He has sacrificed, in the first place, the pleasure of using his money as fast as he earned it upon his daily wants and amusements, and, in the second place, he has sacrificed the time which he has spent in cultivating his allotment; and, moreover, he has saved the money which he paid as rent and that which he put into the bank. So it is to his sacrifice and his saving that he owes his capital.

In just the same way the farmer sacrifices time and labour to raising his crop of wheat, and at the end of the year, when the harvest is gathered, he saves enough from the produce of the year to enable him to sow his field again in the following spring, and thus to raise another crop.

The Capital of a Railway Company

It very often happens nowadays that, in order to carry on some work which requires a great capital, a number of people club their money together and form what is called a *company* to carry on the work. It is in this way that the great railway companies, such as the North-Western, the Great Western Railway, the Midland Railway, and the Great Northern Railway, have been formed, and the persons who have clubbed together to supply the money for making and working these great lines are called the "shareholders."

If the company be successful and a profit is made by working it, then a share of such profit goes to each of the shareholders in proportion to the amount of the capital which he has contributed. If no profit be made, then all the shareholders will be losers, the one who has the most shares of course losing the most, for he will have spent the largest sum of money without getting any return for it. You will see in the chapter further on in this book, headed "Co-operation," how this plan of clubbing together to obtain a large amount of capital has been used with very great success by those who possess but little money.

SUMMARY

CAPITAL

1. Capital is the result of saving and sacrifice.

2. Capital takes many forms. It may take the form of money, of machinery, of land, of houses, of experience, of learning, or of some special knowledge or accomplishment.

3. The value of capital is sometimes increased or diminished by circumstances over which the owner of the capital has no control.

4. The capital necessary to carry on any business may belong to one man, or may be *subscribed* by a number of persons.

Part III

HOW TO LIVE UNDER THE LAW

"DISTRIBUTION SHALL UNDO EXCESS,
AND EACH MAN HAVE ENOUGH."

Shakespeare.

"ALMOST ALL THE ADVANTAGES WHICH
MAN POSSESSES ABOVE THE INFERIOR
ANIMALS, ARISE FROM HIS POWER OF ACTING
IN COMBINATION WITH HIS FELLOWS;
AND OF ACCOMPLISHING BY THE UNITED
EFFORTS OF NUMBERS WHAT COULD NOT BE
ACCOMPLISHED BY THE DETACHED EFFORTS
OF INDIVIDUALS."

J. S. Mill.

CHAPTER XI

CO-OPERATION BETWEEN LABOUR AND CAPITAL

XXXVI

You know I told you that many of the common actions of our life were governed by laws which it was our business to try and understand, and our interest to obey. In the last chapters we have seen what some of these laws are, and how they concern us: I am now coming to a new question.

You remember that I said that although it was dangerous to break, or to act contrary to, the laws of nature and reason and the laws of the land, it was a very good thing to take advantage of them, and to act in obedience to them. We talked in the last chapter of capital and its uses, and of how capital was obtained, and made use of, and we saw that all these things were regulated by laws. In this and the succeeding chapters you will find some examples of how, by living under these laws, obeying them, and acting in accordance with them, we may obtain great advantages for ourselves and others.

The Uses of Capital

I have told you some of the chief uses of capital. In the first place, those who possess capital are able to wait for a return for the money that they have spent, and are not compelled, as the saying goes, "to live from hand to mouth." Again, those who possess capital are able to buy what they want in large quantities, and by so doing to avoid the expense of a great deal of extra work.

Saving of Labour

For instance, if you are laying down coals for the winter, it is cheaper to order a whole cartload at a time than to have the coal brought half a load at a time, in two different journeys, for the cartage will have to be paid on both journeys, and its cost will have to be added to the cost of the coal.

Best Distribution of Work

Then, again, the possession of capital enables a man to distribute the work he requires to have done in the most advantageous manner. It would take one man a very long time to make a coat, for even supposing that he were a real "Jack-of-all-trades," he would have to shear the sheep, to wash, to dye, and to comb the wool, to spin it and to weave it, to cut out the coat, to fit and to stitch it, and long before he had done half this, he would probably be going in rags.

Saving of Time

But the man who possesses capital can obtain the cloth he requires in a much shorter time. He can divide the work which has to be done, among a number of workers, giving to each the task for which he is specially fitted. The wool he will buy from a farmer, the washing, the dyeing, the combing, the spinning, and the weaving will be done in a large factory, by men or women who are specially skilled in each particular branch of cloth-making; and lastly, he will pay a tailor to do the cutting out and fitting.

Saving of Cost

Again, the possession of capital enables a man to buy what he wants at the cheapest price. Take the example of a manufacturer of iron. If he has no capital, or very little capital, he is obliged to buy only sufficient iron to supply the orders which he may have at any given time. If the price of iron be high, he will be obliged, nevertheless, to pay that price, and thus he will be compelled either to sell what he makes at a higher price than he otherwise would have done, or else to keep to the same price and to lose by so doing.

On the other hand, the manufacturer who has a large capital is able to wait until the price of iron is very low, and then, by means of the capital he possesses, to buy a very large quantity at the low price. Then, however much the price of iron may go up afterwards, instead of losing he will gain; for he will be able to make articles at a cheap rate which others can only make at a great cost. These are some examples of the value of capital, and in the chapters which have gone before you will find many others.

It has generally been the rule that those who possessed capital were few, and those who received employment by means of it were many. For instance, a great linen factory or a great iron-foundry often belongs to one or two persons who own the capital, and the work in the factory or the iron-foundry is usually done by a very large number of workers, who receive payment in the shape of wages from the owner of capital.

XXXVII

Profits, and Who Gets Them

Whatever is made out of the business is divided into two shares: one share goes to the owner of the capital, and is called his *profit,* the remainder goes to the workmen, and is called their *wages.* Of course, the share of the workmen, no less than the share of the employer, must really come out of the *profits* of the business, for if it were to come out of the capital, in a very short time there would be no share either for the employer or for the workers; it would be like killing the goose with the golden eggs.

Labour and Capital

In order to obtain the profit at all, it is necessary that the owner of the capital, that is to say the employer, and the owner of the labour, that is to say the workers, should join and work together, or, to use another word, should co-operate. It is by the co-operation between capital and labour that most of the work of the world is done.

As I told you, it usually happens that the owners of the capital and the owners of the labour are different people. But if you think a little, you will *see* that there is no reason why this should always be so. There is no reason why those who give the work should not also supply the capital. As a matter of fact, it generally happens that those who work for wages do not possess much capital, and therefore they are unable really to provide both capital and labour.

But a big building may be made of small bricks. Suppose there are a thousand workers, and that each of them possesses only a very small capital, say six or seven pounds, which would represent a saving of half-a-crown a week out of his weekly wages. Certainly no one of the thousand could hope with such a small sum to enter upon a great business which required two or three thousand pounds a year to work it properly.

But multiply six by one thousand, and straightway instead of six pounds you have six thousand pounds, which is a very different figure. We are all accustomed to the workers "co-operating" in the matter of their labour, and we see how each little piece of good work helps to build up or produce some great work, which no one of the workers alone could possibly have created.

It is not surprising that people should go further, and learn a lesson from labour which can be applied with good results to capital. Is it not possible to co-operate in the matter of capital no less than in the matter of labour? Certainly it is, and it is to enable this kind of co-operation to be undertaken with the greatest chance of success, that the great *Co-operative Societies* have been formed in this country.

In the next chapter I shall tell you something about these Societies: what is the work which they do, what is the principle upon which they are conducted, and how far they may be expected to be of use and profit to those who belong to them.

SUMMARY

CO-OPERATION BETWEEN LABOUR AND CAPITAL

1. Capital helps (*a*) to save labour, (*b*) to save time, (*c*) to save expense.

2. The *profits* of a business are divided between the owners of the capital and the owners of the labour.

3. When the owners of the labour are also the owners of the capital, they receive the share of the profits due to capital as well as that due to labour.

4. Co-operative Societies furnish an example of the owners of the labour being also the owners of the capital.

CHAPTER XII

CO-OPERATIVE SOCIETIES

XXXVIII

All for Each, and Each for All

I TOLD you in the last chapter that for carrying on any large business it was necessary that there should be *"co-operation"* between labour and capital, and I showed that though as a rule the owners of the capital and the owners of the labour are different persons, there is no reason why this should always be the case, but that, on the contrary, there is nothing to prevent the workers themselves supplying the capital needed to make their work successful.

You will remember, too, that the money that is made in a business is divided into two shares, one of which goes to the employer or owner of the capital, and is called his profit, the other to the workers or owners of the labour, and which is called their wages.

Sharing the Profits

Suppose, however, that the worker and the employer are the same person, that is to say, suppose that those who do the work are also those who own the capital, then who will take the two shares I have spoken of? Plainly both shares will go to the workers, one share which will be due to them as workers, in the shape of WAGES, the other share which will be due to them as owners of the capital, in the shape of PROFIT.

In order to allow workers to obtain both the wages earned and the profit made by their work, societies have been formed, which are called "Co-operative Societies."[17] Some of the Societies are so great and important, and the work which they do, if rightly conducted, is so valuable, that it is well worth while to try and understand something of their nature and objects.

How Co-operative Societies Obtain Capital

If ten, or a hundred, or a thousand persons agree to carry on business together, and to share the profits of the business, they must set to work and find the capital for their undertaking. If the capital consists of money, and none of those who agree together are rich men, there is only one way in which it can be obtained, that is by clubbing together and each person subscribing a little. By so doing a large sum of money may be raised.

And this is what the Co-operative Societies in fact do. They begin by requiring all their members either to pay, or promise to pay when required, a small sum, which is expended in buying the material for the work which is to be done; in hiring or building premises in

[17]*Co-operation*—from the Latin *co*, together, and *operatio*, working = working together.

which it may be carried on, in paying proper persons to manage it, and for a variety of other purposes of a similar kind.

Of course it will depend upon the kind of business which is to be carried on, whether the sum required be large or small. There are some kinds of work which require less capital in the shape of money than others—such, for instance, as decorating and painting. In such a trade as that the capital consists for the most part in the skill and cleverness of each worker, and a large sum of money is not

A CO-OPERATIVE SOCIETY

required to enable those who engage in it to go to work. Other businesses require the expenditure of very large sums before they can be expected to return any profit.

For instance, a cotton mill, or a large shop, cannot be started without the payment of thousands of pounds. The building must be bought or hired, the machinery in the mill, and all the stock in the shop, must be purchased, taxes must be paid, the premises must be insured against loss by fire, and a great many other things must be paid for before any work can be done, or any profit made. Hence, a large amount of capital must be provided by those who join together to work a mill or to keep up a large shop.

But whether the sum required be large or small, the way in which it is obtained by Co-operative Societies is the same. It is obtained by all those who belong to the Society joining together to provide the capital, in the hope of sharing, in return, the whole value of the capital, both as wages and as profits.

There are in this country Co-operative Societies for carrying on each of the three trades of which I have already spoken—that of painting and decorating, that of cotton spinning, and that of selling goods retail, or, in other words, keeping a shop.

XXXIX

Different Kinds of Co-operation

There are many other trades which are carried on by Co-operative Societies, but they all of them belong to one of the three classes represented by those referred to. I want you, therefore, to understand what is the difference between these three occupations of decorating, cotton-spinning, and keeping shop. If you understand this clearly, you will be able to follow what I shall say further on about the different forms of co-operation.

A Skilled Co-operative Society

What is the capital which is most needed by a clever decorator and painter? Is it money? No, certainly not. Give an artist a thousand pounds, or ten thousand pounds, and he will not be able to paint any the better for it. Is it labour? No, certainly not. If a man be employed to do work because he is specially skilful in performing it, it is no good giving that man a hundred workmen less skilful than himself to help him in his work. On the contrary, the moment others are allowed to interfere with his work its value is diminished or gone.

No; the capital of such a man is his brains, his skill, his artistic knowledge. His skill and his knowledge of art may have been improved by careful work and preparation, but whether they are gifts given by Nature, or possessions acquired by practice, they equally form his capital.

When, therefore, any number of persons associate themselves together to carry on a trade such as the one we have been speaking about, a trade which requires great skill and taste, and which depends very little, if at all, upon anything else, each person brings into the Society a different amount of capital, which varies in amount according to the skill and knowledge of the particular member. A Society composed of such men as these I shall call a "SKILLED CO-OPERATIVE SOCIETY."

A Productive Co-operative Society

Next we come to the cotton-mill. Where a number of men and women join together for the purpose of carrying on a manufacture such as cotton-spinning, they have to contribute two things—(1) their work, (2) a sufficient amount of capital to enable them to buy or hire the mill, to pay rates and taxes, to purchase the cotton or other material which is to be manufactured, and to keep the mill going in bad times when there is no profit to be made.

As a rule, those who co-operate for such an object as this intend to do like other manufacturers; that is to say, they make their goods as cheap as they can, and sell them for the best price they can get. As a reward for their labour and their sacrifice, they hope to obtain (1) the share of the profit which is paid in wages, and which they would have received if they had not been members of a Co-operative Society, (2) the share of the profits which goes to the owner of the capital, and which, if the factory had not belonged to a Co-operative Society, would have gone to the employer.

The members of such a Society do not as a rule manufacture articles for their own use only. They do not, for instance, only make cotton goods for their own wear, but they buy and sell like other manufacturers. Their business is to produce materials, and to obtain for themselves the whole of the profit of what their labour and their capital produces. Such Societies, therefore, I shall call "Productive Co-operative Societies."

Some Difficulties to be Met

Several Societies of this kind have been formed abroad, and some have been formed in England. Hitherto the success of Productive Co-operative Societies has not been very great. Their failure is usually caused by their members beginning without enough capital, by not having sufficient confidence in their manager or in themselves, or by neglecting to observe the rules which are necessary in all business, whether conducted by a Co-operative Society or not.

There is scarcely any business in which trade does

not vary from time to time, sometimes good and sometimes bad. When trade is bad, an employer begins to lose a part of his profit, and his loss often goes on for a long time before the wages of those who work for him are diminished.

Members of a Productive Co-operative Society are sometimes inclined to forget that they are in the position of both employer and workers, and that they must therefore expect to lose part of their profits when trade is bad. At a time when other workers around them are still receiving the same wages as before, they will be compelled to give up a portion of the share which they have been accustomed to receive.

Bad Times

Thus it is that members of such a Society feel the effects of bad trade very soon. Moreover, it is often impossible in bad times for a Productive Co-operative Society to go on working at all. An employer who has large capital of his own is often compelled to carry on his works for a time without making any profit, or indeed at a loss. He is able to do this because he has saved enough, or has in some way obtained sufficient money, to allow him to wait until times improve.

In a Co-operative Society, however, where the capital is made up of the small subscriptions of all the members, it often happens that though there is enough money to carry on the business when times are prosperous and business is good, there is not enough to keep all the members of the Society in bad times, when no profit is being made.

Bad Management

Again, there is another danger which besets a Productive Co-operative Society. Suppose a thousand persons form a Society for working a cotton-mill. It will be necessary for them to choose certain persons to give orders, to make bargains, and to manage the business. It may be that all the thousand members have an equal share in the mill and an equal interest in its success, but if the whole thousand were to attempt to give orders, to make bargains, and to carry on the business in the way each thought best, you can easily imagine that hopeless confusion would soon be the result. Therefore, it is necessary to appoint one or two persons to do these things.

Now, making bargains and managing a large mill require great experience, knowledge, and skill, and these are qualities which few people possess. As I told you in Chapter VIII, work for which there is a great demand, and which can only be done by few persons, will command a high price, and the case I have given you is no exception to the rule. The man who is chosen by the members of a Co-operative Society to conduct their business must be well paid, or else he is not likely to be a really experienced and clever manager.

Of course, I do not mean to say that men who receive a small sum for their services are not as a rule both clever and honest, but you may depend upon it that so great is the value of experience and knowledge of the kind I have been speaking of, that there will always be plenty of people ready to pay a high price for it.

Now, every one will work for the best wages he can get, and unless a Co-operative Society is willing to pay its managers as well as other manufacturers do, they are not likely to be able to get the best men to do their work.

Want of Promptness

And, lastly, it is most important in the conduct of a great business that those who manage it should be able to act with decision and rapidity. Good bargains are often lost and great opportunities missed by indecision and lack of readiness. It is therefore most important that the members of a Society should give full power to those who manage their business to act promptly and without hesitation. The wisest thing to do is to have men at the outset who are thoroughly honest and able, and to trust them fully.

If the members of the Society do not do this, if they are disheartened by every little failure, and begin at once to find fault with their managers, to give them advice to prevent them acting according to their own judgment and experience, then you may be sure that the way is being prepared for further misfortunes. You know the old proverb that "Too many cooks spoil the broth." It is certainly true in such a case as this, for it is impossible that a great manufacturing business should be conducted by a hundred different people who have to agree together upon every point before any bargain is made or any order given.

How to Overcome the Difficulties

I have mentioned these difficulties which beset Productive Co-operative Societies, because in practice they have been found to be very serious ones, and many of the failures of such Societies have been caused by them. In order that a Co-operative Society which carries on a trade should succeed, its members ought to bear in mind the fact that they are really in the position of any other employer of labour, and that in order to be successful they must follow the same rules, must make the same sacrifices, and take the same precautions as other employers engaged in the same business do.

They must save against bad times, they must be content with small profits when trade is bad, and sometimes with no profits; they must pay their managers well, and, when they have appointed them, they must trust them. It may sometimes be hard to do all these things, but unless they are done the Society will fail.

A Successful Society

Luckily there are some cases in which these truths have already been learnt and laid to heart, and, as a consequence, it is possible to point to Productive Co-operative Societies in this country which have already had a great success, and which seem likely to prosper in the future.

XL

A Distributive Co-operative Society

And now we come to the third great division of the Co-operative Societies. The first was the "Skilled," the second was the "Productive," and the third and the most important is the "Distributive Co-operative Society." That is a long name, no doubt, but it is a very easy one to understand.

As by a Productive Co-operative Society we meant a Society where members worked together to *produce* or make goods, so a Distributive Co-operative Society is one whose members work together to *distribute* or sell goods.

Perhaps the pleasantest and easiest way of explaining to you the nature and objects of such a Society is to give you an account of one of the best known Co-operative Societies.

The Rochdale Equitable Pioneers was one of the first successful Co-operative Societies in this country. It has now become one of the greatest and best known. Its history is full of interest, and shows at every step how much good may be done by honest, resolute, clear-headed men, who understand the difficulties they have to fight against, and who know the true means of overcoming them.

When the Society was formed in the town of Rochdale in the year 1843, times were hard, and the lot of the Lancashire workers was a very hard one. A few of them, however, were able to look forward and to see better times in store for those who were prepared to become "Co-operators," and to give effect to the great idea "of all for each and each for all."

This is an account of how the great Society of the Rochdale Pioneers began, given almost in the words of one of its members, who has done much since that time to bring about the great success which it has now obtained:—

"At the close of the year 1843 a few poor weavers out of employ, and nearly out of food, and quite out of heart with the state of things around them, met together to discover what they could do to better their condition. Manufacturers had capital, shopkeepers had large stocks of goods—how could they succeed without either? Should they go to the workhouse? No; that would mean being dependent on others. Should they emigrate? Not while they could live honestly in their old home. What should they do?

"They would begin the battle of life on their own account. They would learn to do without shop-owners, mill-owners, or owners of capital. They who had neither experience, knowledge, nor money would themselves turn merchants and manufacturers." A subscription list was handed round. A dozen of those present put down a weekly subscription of *twopence each.*

Then they drew up their rules and framed their Society. They declared their object to be to make all members of the Society richer and happier.[18] This was a great object to aim at, and they laid down great plans for its attainment.

But whatever might come in the future, they had to consider the present; the future might have great things in store, the present was made up of very little things. There were twenty-eight members, and they had twenty-eight pounds among them. Whatever the end might be, their business was to make a beginning, and that beginning must be a little one.

However, the Pioneers were practical men, and if they could not do all they wanted, that was no reason why they should not do all that they could. They set to work and established a *Store* for members where no credit was to be given, and where all the profits were to be divided among the members according to the purchases they had made.

But £28 does not go far.

They set up business in a ground-floor room in *Toad Lane*, Rochdale, and the whole amount of the goods in the shop was worth only £15. The neighbours laughed at them, and some ill-natured people prophesied all sorts of evil things of them and their work. But after a time the neighbours ceased laughing, and joined the Society;

[18] "The objects and plans of this Society are to form arrangements for the pecuniary benefit and the improvement of the social and domestic condition of its members."

THE OLD HOME OF THE ROCHDALE PIONEERS,
IN TOAD LANE

and the evil prophecies did not come true. In 1843 there were eighty members, and the weekly takings had reached £30.

In 1848 bad times came in Lancashire, and many new members joined in order to get the benefits of the Society. In 1847 a drapery business was added to the grocery. In 1852 shoemaking was begun, and year by year, as the Society grew in numbers and increased in prosperity, new branches were opened, until at the present time there are over twenty branches in Rochdale, and more than 10,000 members.

The history of this great Society will serve as an example of the third and perhaps the most important kind of Co-operative Society. It is a *Distributive* Society, whose object, as its name shows, is to *distribute* to members or purchasers articles which are bought in large quantities. In other words, it is a great *retail establishment.*

THE NEW HOME OF THE ROCHDALE PIONEERS

SUMMARY

CO-OPERATIVE SOCIETIES

1. The capital of Co-operative Societies is obtained from the small subscriptions of a great number of persons who are members of the Society.

2. There are various kinds of Co-operative Societies, including (*a*) Skilled Co-operative Societies, (*b*) Productive Co-operative Societies, (*c*) Distributive Co-operative Societies.

3. Members of a Co-operative Society in order to be successful must observe the same rules of business as other owners of capital.

CHAPTER XIII

THE ADVANTAGES OF CO-OPERATION

XLI

What is the Good of It?

LET us see what are the advantages which belong to such a Society as that named in the last chapter. The chief advantages which the customers of a Co-operative Society get are low prices and good quality. All that they buy is cheap and good. How is it that Co-operation enables people to sell the best articles at the lowest prices? There are several explanations.

In the first place, the members of a Co-operative Society get all the advantage which is conferred by the possession of capital. We saw in the chapter on Capital what some of these advantages were. In the first place, the owner of a large capital can buy when he likes and where he likes. Here is an example of what has sometimes happened, and which shows how great an advantage it may be to be able to choose the time for making a purchase.

J. Brown and W. Smith,
or the Man who could Afford to Wait

James Brown and William Smith were both tobacconists; Brown had a large capital, Smith had none. Both of them, of course, were compelled to make purchases of tobacco from time to time to keep up their stock. One day it was rumoured about that a fresh tax was to be placed upon tobacco by Parliament, and that instead of all tobacco having to pay a tax of 3s. 6d. a pound it would soon have to pay 3s. 6½d. a pound.

On hearing of this, Brown, having a large sum of money ready to hand, at once bought enough tobacco at the old price to keep up his stock for another twelve months. William Smith could not afford to do this; he had no capital, and was only able to buy fresh tobacco every month out of the profit he had made in the month before. He was obliged to wait, and as soon as the new tax was voted by Parliament he was obliged to pay an extra halfpenny for every pound he bought.

Now here, you see, were Brown and Smith both selling just the same article, but in the sale of it Brown had a great advantage. He might do one of two things: either he might charge a halfpenny a pound more to his customers for all the tobacco they bought, in which case each halfpenny would be a clear profit to him over and above what he got before, or else he might go on selling the tobacco at the old price.

It is clear that he would not lose any money by doing this, for by buying all his tobacco before the tax was raised he was put to no extra expense. But not only would he lose nothing, but he would be very certain to gain.

What would be the position of William Smith? He would either have to go on selling at the old price, in which case he would lose a halfpenny out of the profit he formerly made on each pound, or else he would have to put on a halfpenny to the price charged to his customers.

Now, you may be sure the moment many of Smith's customers found that they were paying a halfpenny more for the very same thing that Brown was selling at the old price, many would leave Smith for Brown, and so the latter would soon gain in another way. Thus you will see how great an advantage came to Brown from being able to buy when he liked.

XLII

The Advantages of Capital to a Society

It is this advantage that the members of a Co-operative Society are able to secure for themselves. By clubbing their money together they are able to supply capital to those who manage the Society, and these in their turn are able to use it to the best advantage and to make purchases at the best time.

Then, by co-operation the members of a Society can obtain another advantage which comes from the possession of capital. Not only can they buy *when* they like, but they can also buy *where* they like.

Perhaps some of you have looked at the strange phrases which appear in the newspapers under the heading of "Commercial Intelligence." There you will often see such passages as the following:—

"London.—Sugar is firm. Beet dearer. Cheese and bacon quiet and unchanged." This means that the price of sugar in London remains steady, that beet-root, from which sugar is largely made, is dearer, and that there is little demand for cheese and bacon, the prices of which have therefore not gone up. Plainly this is the time for any one who wants a large quantity of cheese and bacon to buy it in London, where it is cheap, and it is a bad time for him to buy beet-root there, because it is expensive.

At the same time suppose a merchant has undertaken to supply a thousand tons of beet-root to a purchaser in Paris; when he finds that the article he wants is so dear in London, he will look round and see if it can be got cheaper somewhere else. Perhaps he finds that in the south of France at Marseilles, or in the North of Germany at Hamburg, there are large quantities of beet-root waiting to be sold, with few people to buy them, and that in consequence "Beet" in these places is "easier" or "quieter"—that is to say, cheaper than in London; he will then naturally find it to his advantage to buy the amount he requires at the lower price in Marseilles or Hamburg, and to send it thence to Paris: while at the same time he buys his cheese and his bacon in London, where they are cheap, instead of in Hamburg or Marseilles, where they are dear.

But all this he can only do if he has capital enough to buy at once the exact quantity he requires, at the exact place where it is cheapest and best. The members of a Co-operative Society have this capital, and by entrusting its management to experienced and trustworthy men they get the benefit of it.

Then, again, one of the greatest advantages which the owner of capital possesses is that he is able to pay ready money, or "cash," as it is usually called, for what he buys.

Ready Money

There are only two ways in which a man who has not capital can buy large quantities of goods, and in either case he will have to pay something more than the actual cost of what he buys. In the first place, he may borrow the money, and pay it down in cash to the man from whom he buys. He will then, it is true, get the advantage of ready-money payment; but, on the other hand, he will have to pay back the money he borrowed, and not only what he borrowed, but interest for the use of it.

Or he may obtain the goods he requires without paying ready-money, or, as it is called, on credit. In that case he will be no better off than he was before, for instead of paying interest upon what he borrowed, he will have to pay interest on the debt which he owes for the goods. So either way he will have to pay, not only the cost of what he buys and receives, but something over and beyond in the shape of interest.

The position of such a man must plainly be worse than that of another engaged in the same business who pays "cash" for all he buys. The latter buys cheaper, and therefore can afford to sell cheaper. And so it is with the members of a Co-operative Society; by subscribing together they are able to pay "cash," and therefore to buy cheap.

XLIII

Buying Wholesale

Then, again, there is another great advantage which is gained by Co-operation, and which is the result of buying and selling very great quantities, or, as it is called, "wholesale," instead of dealing only with small amounts and few customers.

Mr. Careful and the Co-operative Society

Take a single street in which there are a number of shops of different kinds—a grocer, a butcher, a tailor, a shoemaker, a stationer, a baker, and others. Those who live in the neighbourhood must of course be supplied with meat, bread, groceries, boots and shoes, and clothes; and to get all these things they will go to each of the different shops, and they will have to pay in each case the price which the shopkeeper is compelled in his own interest to charge.

But what will that price be? Will it be the real cost of the bread, the meat, the tea and sugar, the boots, or the coats which are sold?

Certainly not. Let us take the case of the butcher. We will call him Mr. Cleaver. He is perhaps a man with a family, whom he must support, and occupying a house for which he must pay rent. He must therefore put the price of his meat sufficiently high to allow him to pay the man from whom he buys it, and also to save a profit for his own expenses, his house-rent, and the maintenance of his family.

But that is by no means the end of it. For in small shops it very often happens that the meat is not bought directly from the man to whom the oxen and sheep belonged in the first instance. In very many cases the butcher buys from a wholesale dealer—a middle-man, as he is sometimes called.

Mr. Turner the middle-man, like Mr. Cleaver the butcher, and indeed like everybody else who has to conduct a business, must make a profit, for he too has a home to keep up, and maybe a family to support, besides having to pay Mr. Furrow the farmer, from whom he buys the oxen and sheep which he sells as beef and mutton.

Just as Mr. Cleaver, therefore, had to add on something to the price at which he bought the meat from the middle-man in order to make a profit, so in his turn must Mr. Turner add on something to the price charged to the butcher over and above what he himself paid to the farmer.

And, indeed, that is not the end of the story. For Mr. Furrow the farmer has not only to repay himself for the expense of feeding and keeping the cattle until they come to market, but he in his turn must pay his rent to Mr. Acres, his landlord, must keep a home over his head, and must pay the expenses of himself and Mrs. Furrow, and all the Master and Miss Furrows, if there be any. To do this he must make a profit, and to make a profit he must charge Mr. Turner for the cattle something over and above the price which he himself paid for keeping and feeding them.

Now you will see that there are *four profits* to be paid. First there is Mr. Cleaver the butcher; secondly, there is Mr. Turner the middle-man; thirdly, there is Mr. Furrow the farmer; and lastly, there is Mr. Acres the landlord. It is plain that Mr. Furrow pays Mr. Acres' profit, it is equally certain that Mr. Cleaver pays Mr. Turner's profit and that of Mr. Acres into the bargain, and who is it pays Mr. Cleaver's profit? That is a question you can soon answer—it is Mr. Careful, the customer who buys the leg of mutton in Mr. Cleaver's shop, who pays it, and in doing so pays not only the butcher's profit, but the middleman's profit, and the farmer's, and the landlord's.

One Man instead of Five

Now suppose the owner of the land, the farmer, the middle-man, the butcher, and the purchaser of the leg of mutton, *instead of being five different people are one* and the same person, then it is plain that instead of the profit upon the meat being divided among four different people, it will all go to one person, and that one the purchaser who gets the leg of mutton.

And this, or something like it, is what happens in the case of a member of a great Distributive Co-operative Society. For each member who buys goods from the Society is also the owner of a share of the capital with which the Society purchases the goods, and therefore not only does he obtain the advantage as purchaser of being able to buy good articles at reasonable prices from the Society, but as seller he gets a share of the profit which is made upon all the articles which are sold.

XLIV

Where Co-operators get the Advantage

I have now explained to you some of the advantages which are gained by belonging to a Co-operative Society, and why it is that members are able to buy better and cheaper than if they had no means of working together.

I have shown you how by co-operation they obtain the use of capital, and how the use of capital brings with it the power to buy in large quantities, to buy at the most favourable time and in the most favourable place, to pay ready-money, and therefore to buy cheap, to buy direct from those who supply the goods, and thus to avoid paying a profit to several persons, such as the farmer, the middle-man, and the butcher in the illustration I gave you.

There are other advantages which are to be gained by co-operation, such as cheapness of management, convenience and cleanliness in storing and keeping goods, and other matters.

But the principal advantages are those which have been mentioned. They are indeed very great, and furnish a strong reason why those who desire to save money, and at the same time to get good value for the money they spend, should become members of such societies.

Two Ways of Profit Sharing

There are two ways in which those who belong to Co-operative Societies may share the profit which is made by buying and selling. It is necessary to understand what these two ways are. We saw that such Societies were able to secure great advantages in carrying on their trade by the use of capital, and that among other things they were enabled to buy the goods they sold to their customers at a very low price.

Now the buyers are the customers, and the customers are the buyers, and the customers have a right to share the profit which is made on their behalf. There are two ways in which they can do this.

Either they can fix the price of each article they buy at a very low figure, and thus share the profit by buying very cheap that which they would otherwise have had to pay a high price for;

Or else they can fix the prices at exactly the same figure as other people do who do not get the advantages of their capital, and can afterwards divide the profit which is made out of all the purchases from the Society in the course of the year.

XLV

The History of some Sugar

The easiest way to explain what I mean is by way of an example—

In a certain town there were two places where sugar could be obtained. One of these places belonged to the members of a Co-operative Society, the other did not. The Society possessed the advantages I told you of; it had capital and credit, and was able to make its purchases when it chose and where it chose.

As Christmas drew near both establishments in the town had to lay in a stock of sugar, in order to be ready for all the buyers who were sure to want sugar to put into their plum puddings and cakes.

The managers of the Co-operative Society at once ordered one of their men to find out the place in which sugar was to be got best and cheapest, and he soon reported to them that there were two whole shiploads of sugar in the docks at Liverpool, which they could buy at 2d. per lb., provided they paid ready-money and bought a whole cargo. The managers agreed to this, and the whole of one cargo of sugar was bought.

But the other seller of sugar was not so fortunate; he was unable either to buy a whole cargo at a time, or to pay so large a sum in ready-money. The sugar out of the other ship, therefore, was divided up and sold in lots in Liverpool to "brokers," who in their turn sold it to merchants, and the merchants again divided it into smaller portions and sold it to dealers, or persons who bought it to sell to smaller shopkeepers; and lastly, the particular shopkeeper of whom I have been telling you, bought the amount of sugar he required in this way from a dealer.

How the Profit was Made

Now you may be quite sure that all these people who had bought and sold the sugar before it got to the shop had not done their work for nothing. Like the landlord, the farmer, the middle-man, and the butcher, they had each of them made a profit upon the sugar as it passed through their hands.

And so by the time it got finally to the sellers, the sugar, instead of costing 2d. per lb., cost 3d. per lb., or ld. more than it cost the members of the Cooperative Society. Now one penny is not a large sum, but multiply by 100 and it becomes 8s. 4d., and multiply again by 100 and you will have a sum like this 8s. 4d. x 100 = £41 13s. 4d.

Now you will see that if the two sellers had charged their customers for the sugar precisely what they each gave for it, 100 lb. of sugar sold by the Co-operative Society would have cost 8s. 4d. less than 100 lb. sold at the shop. But of course the owner of the shop was not contented with selling the sugar at the price which he paid for it. He had to make a profit. He therefore put up in his window, "Best sugar 4d. per lb." In this way he was sure to make a profit of 1d. on every pound of sugar sold.

How shall the Profit be Shared?

The managers of the Co-operative Society now had to decide what price they should put upon *their* sugar. There were two opinions as to what was the wisest course to pursue.

Plan Number One

"Let us," said one of the members, "sell all our sugar at 2d. a lb. It is true that we shall get no profit in money by doing so, but at the same time every member who buys a pound of sugar from us at 2d. instead of at 4d. a lb. from the shop, will keep 2d. in his pocket, and will be a richer man by that amount. What he saves on his sugar he will be able to spend upon tea, or clothes, or presents for his friends.

"Besides, look what an advantage it will give us over the shop; for who will buy sugar for 4d. a lb. when for 2d. he can get the very same thing from the Society?"

Plan Number Two

"No," said another of the managers. "I do not think that is the wisest way. Let us sell our sugar for the same price as it is sold at in the shop, and you will see that we shall make a very large profit. For instead of gaining only ld. in every pound we shall gain 2d., which will all go to the good of the Society. When we have made this profit we will distribute it in money among the members of the Society."

"But how," said another, "will you distribute it justly? It is not fair that a member who has bought nothing

T ADVS OF COOPER

from the Society should grow rich at the expense of others." "Certainly, that would be most unfair," replied the former. "What I propose is this, that to every member of the Society who buys any sugar should be given a ticket saying how much he had bought, and what he paid for it.

"Then when all is sold, every one who has bought sugar will present his ticket to us, and we shall give him a share in the profits according to the amount which he has paid towards them. The more a man has paid the more he will receive.

"In this way the profits will be fairly distributed, and every one will be inclined to buy from us when he knows that the more he buys the more profit will in the end come back to him."

SUMMARY

THE ADVANTAGES OF CO-OPERATION

1. Co-operative Societies have an advantage in possessing capital, for they are able (*a*) to wait and buy at the best time and in the best place; (*b*) to pay ready money; (*c*) to buy wholesale.

2. Co-operators may share their profits in various ways—for instance, they may (*a*) sell the articles they deal in at a low price to their members, thus enabling the latter to save the difference between cheap and dear goods; or (*b*) they may sell at the same prices as other people, and divide the profits they receive among the members of the Society.

175

CHAPTER XIV

TRADES UNIONS

XLVI

What Trades Unions are

I SUPPOSE there are very few people who have not, at one time or another, heard of "Trades Unions;" but to hear of a thing and to know exactly what it means, are two very different things. I am going to try and explain to you what Trades Unions are, how they arose, and what is the work which they are formed to do.

A Trades Union is a society formed by men of the same trade, and its object is threefold. Its first object is to obtain work for all its members; its second object is to obtain good wages, shorter hours, and greater comfort for all its members who obtain work; and, lastly, it has usually a third object, which is to support and assist those of its members who are out of work.

Now, these are all very good objects, and as long as they can be obtained honestly and justly they are very well worth all the efforts which the Trades Unions can make to secure them.

Let us see by what means and under what conditions they can really be obtained. You remember what I told you in Chapter V about the laws of nature and of reason, and what I told you in Chapter IV about the laws of England, and how it was both dangerous and wrong to break or disobey either the one or the other.

The rule that I gave you then holds good in the case of the Trades Unions, which we are now speaking about. As long as the members of the Union pursue their end in obedience to the laws of England, and in accordance with the laws of nature and reason, so long will they prosper and be a good and helpful influence in the country; but directly they break either of these laws they become not only harmful and dangerous bodies, but they will labour in vain, for, in the long run, the laws of nature and reason will prevail, even though the law of England fails to punish the offenders.

Many hundreds of thousands of workers in this country belong to Trades Unions, and millions of pounds are collected and spent by the members of the Unions every year.

It is, therefore, most important to try and understand which are the right and wise methods which Trades Unions can adopt in order to gain their threefold object—good work, good wages, and help when work is not to be had.

XLVII

Some Facts about Trades Unions

But, before going any further, it will be best to explain exactly what Trades Unions are, and what, as a general rule, they really do.

A Trades Union is a club or society formed of members of the same trade, who agree together to observe certain rules and to act in certain ways as long as they remain members of the society. The first rule is generally to the effect that each member of the Union shall pay a certain sum at regular intervals to the society. To this is generally added a rule which makes it the duty of the members to pay extra sums at special times, when the society is in need of help.

The Rules, the Managers, and the Money

The rules of different societies vary much in small matters, but in their main points they are much alike. Power is usually given to a small number of the members of the Union to make the necessary rules and to carry on the work.

The members so chosen are elected to their office by all the members, and are called the Council, or Central Committee of the Union. Every member, as long as he remains a member of the Union, binds himself to obey its rules and to support the authority of those who are elected to manage its business.

The money which the Union requires to carry on its work is raised, as I told you, by subscription from the members. Sometimes it is a fixed sum which has to be paid every week or every month, and sometimes it is a sum which varies in amount according to the amount of wages which the member who has to pay it is receiving at the time.

What do Trades Unions do?

Now that we know what Trades Unions are, and also what are the chief objects for which they are formed, it is time to inquire by what means they try to attain these objects, and how far the means they adopt are likely to help them to the ends they seek.

The object of a Trades Union is to obtain work for all its members. This is a very good object, and Trades Unions, if they are well conducted, can generally do a great deal towards attaining it. In the first place, the officers of the Union receive information from all parts of the country, and indeed from all parts of the world, as to whether there be a demand or not in any particular place for the kind of work which members of that Union are able to do.

Work

When they know where there is the greatest demand, they can tell the members of the Union, and if work is slack in one place—in other words, if there is a small demand for their labour—they can go to another place where work is brisk, that is to say, where there is a great demand, and in this way they will obtain wages which they would not have obtained except by the help of the Union.

Good Work

Again, a Trades Union may do what many such societies are nowadays doing: they may take steps to educate and train those who are entering upon the trade with which they are concerned. By so doing they will be rendering their members more valuable assistance than they would otherwise have been, and will fit them to undertake a higher class of work than they would otherwise have been capable of; in other words, they will be increasing the extent of the demand for their work.

In all these cases you will see that the Trades Unions do good by acting in accordance with the laws of Nature and of Reason, of which we spoke in an earlier chapter. They help their members by taking advantage of these laws.

XLVIII

Good Wages and Short Hours

We now come to the second great object which a Trades Union generally strives for, and which consists in obtaining for its members good wages, short hours, and greater comfort. There can be no doubt whatever that all these are very worthy objects indeed, and that every Union which achieves any one of them without doing any injury to others is conferring a great boon upon those who belong to it.

How the Work is Done

There are various ways in which a Trades Union seeks these ends.

In the first place, by uniting a great number of workers together in one body, and enabling them to ask for what they want through the mouth of a few persons who speak in the name of the whole number, the workers who belong to a Trades Union possess a power which those who are outside of it cannot hope to exercise.

Union is Strength

There is a proverb which is the motto of the kingdom of Belgium:—"L'union fait la force," or "Union is strength." There can be no doubt that the demands of men are often listened to with more attention when they are united and organised than when they make their requests separately, and without any agreement.

And by this I do not mean that such bodies obtain what they ask for, or ought to obtain it, because they are so strong that those to whom they appeal are afraid of them.

The moment such a union is used to make people afraid, or to obtain by force what cannot be obtained by reason, it becomes bad and harmful. But, as you will see, there are many ways in which Union is strength; even though it be not used as a threat against anybody.

For instance, supposing the members of a Trades Union believe that their wages are insufficient, or that their hours of labour are too long, they may inform the employers of the fact, and ask them to increase the wages or to shorten the hours.

In some cases it happens that the request of the

workers is supported by such good reasons that the employers will consent at once to make the concession which is asked.

Sometimes of course it happens that the workers and the employers do not agree, and the latter refuse to meet the wishes of the former. In such a case, where reason and argument are exhausted on both sides, and no arrangement has been made, it frequently happens that the members of a Trades Union decide to "strike" to obtain their point.

There have been many "strikes" in this country, and their consequences have often been so serious, and, whether good or evil, have affected so many people, that it is worth while to give up a chapter to explaining what a strike really means, how far it is useful or the contrary, and what are the circumstances under which it generally takes place.

SUMMARY

TRADES UNIONS

1. Trades Unions are societies formed by men of the same trade.

2. The principal objects of a Trades Union are— (*a*) To obtain work for all its members; (*b*) to obtain good wages, shorter hours, and greater comfort for its members; (*c*) to support and assist those of its members who are out of work.

3. Trades Unions ought to act in accordance with the laws of nature and reason.

CHAPTER XV

STRIKES

XLIX

What a Strike is

When a number of workers ask their employer to give them more wages, to shorten their hours, or in some way or other to make the conditions of their work more favourable, and the employer refuses to grant their request, and the workers agree together not to work for the employer at all until he has accepted their terms, the workers are said to strike.

It is not necessary that men should belong to a Trades Union in order to strike; any number of men engaged upon the same piece of work may agree to act together in a certain way towards their employer.

But in order that a strike should be successful, it is necessary that all those who take part in it should act in the same way and at the same time, and it is found in practice that such agreement, and such power of working together, is seldom to be found except among bodies of men who are accustomed to observe regular rules, and to submit to the authority of chosen representatives.

Hence it generally happens that strikes are undertaken by members of Trades Unions, who possess the disciplined spirit of obedience which they have acquired as members of their society.

Of course the object of a strike is to compel the employer to grant the terms of the workers. By refusing to work, the strikers prevent the owner of the capital from making any profit; and not only that, they very often can inflict upon him very great loss.

For instance, if a manufacturer has undertaken to supply one thousand pieces of cloth on a certain day, and while he is still engaged upon making the cloth his workmen strike work, then the consequences may be very serious for him, for when the day comes for delivering the cloth and carrying out his bargain, there will be no cloth forthcoming, and either the manufacturer will be compelled to buy, at his own expense, a sufficient quantity from some other mill to give to his customer, or he will fail altogether to fulfil his bargain, and will be liable to pay for any loss which he may have occasioned to his customer by his failure.

Then, again, there are many kinds of machinery which spoil very fast when they are not in use and are not being looked after, and by refusing to work the strikers can inflict loss upon the employer by diminishing the value of the machinery which forms part of his capital.

By thus exposing the employer to loss and risk, the strikers are enabled to put pressure upon the owner of the capital, and to compel him to listen to their demands.

BUSY TIME IN A MANUFACTURING DISTRICT

If the actual loss to the employer, or even the fear of actual loss, be so great as to lead him to grant what he at first refused, then the strike has been successful, in one respect, at least, though, as I shall show you further on, it sometimes happens that a strike which succeeds in one way, may yet cause so much loss and suffering to those who take part in it, that more is really lost than is won.

If the employer be neither alarmed nor damaged by the strike, and if he thinks that he would suffer more by agreeing to the demands which are made upon him than by allowing his works to be stopped; or if, finally, he finds that he can continue the work without the help of the strikers, then the strike is considered to have failed.

L

Are Strikes Right or Wrong?

It is sometimes asked, Are strikes right or wrong? Certainly, if a strike means nothing more than what I have described to you, it is not wrong. Every man has a right to work or not as he pleases, and he has a perfect right to say, "I will not work at all unless I get better wages," or "unless my hours are shortened," or "unless something be done to make my work safer or more agreeable." If by agreeing with other workers to join him in his requests, he can obtain what he requires more readily, there is certainly nothing wrong in his doing so.

In either case he is only doing what every one else does who is making a bargain—he is trying to get a good price for what he sells—that is, for his labour. But whether he gets what he wants will depend in the long run on the same laws of supply and demand of which you have heard so much.

If there be a demand for the work which he and other members of the Union can do, then he and they will get paid for doing it. If there be a great demand for it, if the demand for it be greater than the supply—that is to say, if enough workers cannot be got to do it unless he and his comrades will undertake it—then probably the strike will succeed, for the employer will be able to afford to pay more for work which is certain to be bought.

If, on the other hand, the demand for the work be small, or if, while the demand be great, the number of workers ready to do it be very large, then as a rule the strike will fail, for an employer will not care to pay for work which he cannot sell, nor will he pay more to the strikers when he can obtain plenty of other men to do the work at the old rate of wages.

The Law of Strikes

Thus, if we examine the matter, we shall see that the laws of supply and demand really govern the question of wages, and that they are not in any way altered by strikes; on the contrary, strikes are regulated by them.

It is often said that it is useless to "strike against a falling market." This sounds a difficult phrase, meant for business men only, but it is not so really, and if you have paid attention to what has gone before in this chapter, you will easily understand it. It simply means that where trade is bad and the demand for a particular kind of work is decreasing, there is very little chance of a strike succeeding, because a time when employers are losing their profits, and perhaps losing their money, is not a time when they are likely to diminish their profit still further, or to increase their loss by paying higher wages for unprofitable work.

It is when trade is improving, and prices are rising, that strikes are likely to succeed, for employers will then have more money to share with the workers, and moreover, they will be afraid to stop their works at a time when everything is beginning to look prosperous, and there is a hope of increasing profits.

I have shown you that as long as strikes are carried on in the way I have described, they are certainly not wrong; but it does not follow that because a thing is not wrong it is necessarily wise to do it.

On the contrary, it is certain that many strikes are not wise at all, and are only brought about by the short-sightedness, or the anger, or the ignorance of those who are the cause of them, whether they be the employers or the workers. I do not say that it is always best to avoid strikes, but certainly many strikes have taken place which have done much more harm than they have good.

LI

Some Facts about Strikes

I said that, very often, strikes which were successful

in bringing about the particular purpose for which they were undertaken, have nevertheless brought more loss than gain to both parties engaged in them. You will easily see how this may be.

For instance, suppose a worker is earning 30s. a week, and that his employer gives him notice that he is going to reduce his wages by 3s. a week, that is to say to 27s. The worker then joins in a strike to prevent his wages being lowered, and after his being for two months on strike the employer gives way and consents to pay 30s. as before.

Let us see how matters will stand then. The worker, by getting his way, will have earned 30s. a week instead of 27s. for ten months out of the year; that is to say, he will have earned £65 in ten months instead of £70 4s. in the twelve months. In other words, instead of gaining anything during the year he will have lost £5 4s.

From this example you will see that there are many matters to be considered before a strike is decided upon, and that even those strikes which appear to be successful, often occasion loss and suffering which it would have been much better to avoid.

Another Side of the Question

There is, however, another side to this question which it is necessary to mention. As I have told you, it sometimes happens that a strike which appears to be successful is really a loss to those who take part in it. On the other hand, it is no less true that some strikes, which seem to have caused very great loss to the strikers, have really been the means of conferring a great advantage upon them, or, at any rate, upon other members of the same trade.

For instance, here is a case that actually happened: 500 men were engaged in a particular trade, and out of the 500, 300 went out on strike for an advance in wages of 2s. a week. After the strike had gone on for three weeks, the employers granted the demands of the strikers, and consented to pay them 32s. a week, instead of 30s. as before.

Let us see what were the gains and losses in this case. The 300 men were on strike for three weeks, and during that time, of course, they lost the whole of their wages, which, at 30s. per week for three weeks, comes to £1,350. It is true that at the end of the three weeks the strike succeeded, and that for the future they received 32s. instead of 30s. But each man had lost 90s., and forty-five weeks would have to pass before this loss was made up.

But two things must be remembered which will give quite another result. In the first place the men on strike belonged to a Trades Union; in the second place, it was not only the 300 who went on strike who got the increase of 2s. a week, but the other 200 workers in the same trade as well.

Now, what difference do these facts make in the sum we have just done? Let us see. In the first place, the strikers, being members of a Trades Union, received from the subscriptions paid by other members of the Union a payment of 10s. a week, under the name of *strike pay,* during the three weeks they were on strike.

Instead, therefore, of losing 30s. a week, each man lost 20s. only, or 60s. for the three weeks, or a total of £900 instead of £1,350. Then, at the end of the three weeks, not only did the strikers begin to receive 32s. instead of 30s., but the other members of the trade as well. Thus, as soon as the strike ended, there were 500 men gaining an additional wage of 2s. a week per man, or £50 a week altogether.

In 20 weeks they had more than made up the £900 which was lost in the strike. In 52 weeks, or one year, they had gained £1,700; and when I tell you that the additional wages gained in this particular strike were paid not for one year only, but for five, you will see that in five years the extra wages earned by these 500 men in consequence of the strike amounted to no less than £12,100 over and above the amount required to repay all the wages lost by the strike.

I have given you this example because it illustrates a case which has really happened, and, indeed, such a success for the strikers has not been uncommon. But the cases in which the suffering and loss and failure outweigh the advantage gained are, without doubt, more frequent. And, as you will see, the larger the number of members in a trade who go out on strike, the smaller will be the chance of a real success.

LII

The Fewer Strikes the Better

On the whole, it is certain that the more often strikes can be avoided the better it will be for workers and employers. And this brings us to a very important question.

What is the best way to avoid strikes and still to obtain the advantages for which a strike is undertaken? This is a question which is often asked, and to which it is most important a wise answer should be given. Perhaps, if we consider the matter, we shall find a good answer.

The Reason Why

We have seen that no demand for a rise in wages is likely to succeed when it is more profitable for the employer to let his works stop than to go on with them and have to pay the higher rate of wages. For instance, supposing a manufacturer employing 500 men makes £3,150 a month, out of which he has to pay the workers and to keep a profit for himself. Let us say that he pays the workers an average wage of 30s. per week, or £6 per month, making £3,000 to be paid in wages, and leaving him £150 profit. Then, if the workers ask him to give them an increase of 2s. a week, how will matters stand?

Two shillings a week is not a very large sum, but 2s. x 500 x 4 = 4,000s., or £200. The employer will thus have to pay £3,200 a month for wages. What, then, will become of his profit of £150? Not only will the profit have disappeared, but in place of it there will be a monthly loss of £50, or £600 a year. Plainly, most men would rather shut up their works altogether than go on working at such a loss, even for a short time.

Some More Figures

Again, supposing the same employer is asked to give an increase, not of 2s. a week, but of only half that sum, that is to say, 1s. And suppose, at the same time his trade, instead of being prosperous as before, is becoming worse and worse, and that at the end of each month he finds himself with £2,800 only instead of £3,150 out of which to pay wages and take a profit.

He will be in just as bad a case as he was in the first instance, for though a smaller increase is asked, there, will be a smaller sum to meet it, and instead of having to meet a payment of £3,000 out of a sum of £3,150, he will have to meet a payment of £3,100 out of a sum of only £2,800.

So you will soon see that in either of these cases a strike would be useless and unwise, for in most cases the employer would rather close his mills than work them at such a loss; or, if he were compelled to give way to the strikers, he could only do so by injuring himself in the first place and injuring the workers in the second, for the increased wages could only be paid out of the employer's capital, and, as soon as the capital went, the business would come to a standstill altogether, and soon, instead of low wages, there would be no wages.

And now, once more, suppose that when the demand for higher wages is made, business is improving, and that, instead of £3,150 a month, the employer finds that he is making £3,750 a month.

Then it is plain that, if he choose to do so, he can afford to pay the extra wages which he is asked for, and, at the same time, not only to retain his former profit of £150 a month, but to get the advantage of the good trade, and to get £400 over and above the £150.

This is a case in which a strike might be successful, for the employer would, of course, rather pay the extra wages than run the risk of losing, not only the additional profit, but all profit.

These cases seem clear enough, and if all real cases were as plain from beginning to end as these are, there would probably be very few strikes, for both employers and workers would know beforehand whether the requests made were reasonable, or whether they could fairly be granted.

LIII

How to Do without Strikes

Is it not possible to think of some means by which disputes as to wages and work can be settled on some such plan as your own common sense helps you to apply in the cases we have just read?

Is it not possible for both sides in such a dispute to find out what are the real facts of the case, and what is just and reasonable, before quarrelling and allowing a strike, with all its inconveniences and dangers, to be begun? Yes, there certainly is a means by which this may be done, and happily many employers and many workers have found it out, and have used it with good effect.

In many parts of England, and, in many trades, disputes as to work and wages are settled by *arbitration,* that is to say, by the decision of one or two fair-minded persons who are appointed by the two sides to hear and examine all the facts, and to decide what is just and right under the circumstances. These persons are called "arbitrators."

The arbitrators are given every information which they require as to the state of the business, the profits of the employer, and all other matters which are necessary to forming a true judgment, and when they have thoroughly considered all sides of the question they give their judgment or award, and whatever it may be, whether in favour of one side or of the other, both sides abide by it.

In some trades, what are called *Councils of Conciliation* have been formed, that is to say, arrangements have been made for always having arbitrators, in whom both employers and workers trust, to whom each question can be referred as soon as it arises.

Help when Out of Work

We have now dealt with two out of the three objects for which I told you Trades Unions are formed. We have seen (1) what methods they adopt in order to obtain wages for all their members; (2) by what means they endeavour to secure good wages, short hours, and greater safety, convenience, or comfort for their members when at work. We now come to the last of the objects I named, (3) that of supporting and assisting members who are out of work.

It very often happens, in all trades, that men are at times out of work, sometimes because trade is bad, sometimes, as in the building trade, because the weather is unfavourable and no work can be done, and for a variety of other reasons. At such times the Trades Unions often undertake to pay a certain sum of

TALKING OVER THE STRIKE

money every week to those who are thus prevented from earning wages. The money is paid out of the subscriptions of all the members, which have been collected for that purpose, and of course only those who have themselves contributed are allowed to receive the benefit of such payments.

By thus helping their members at a time when they are in need of assistance, and when they are suffering through no fault of their own, the Trades Unions are often able to do great good, and to enable honest and willing workers to tide over a bad time without having to break up their homes and lose their position.

Strike Pay

There is one other important time when the Trades Unions pay money to their members that I must not omit to mention. It is when a strike is undertaken with the consent and advice of the Union that the greatest necessity arises for help to those who are out of work.

Many men who live on weekly or daily wages, would very quickly starve if they were to go out on strike; and long before they could hope to bring their employer to accept their terms, they would have to return to work at any rate of wages which he chose to offer them. For however determined a man may be, and however sure he may be of the justice of his demands, he cannot starve himself to death in order to obtain them.

It is with the object therefore of putting the workers upon the same footing as the employers, and of giving them the means of living until their requests are fairly heard and fairly answered, that the Trades Unions give what is called "strike pay" to those who are out of work through having joined a strike,

Sometimes in great strikes, where both sides are very determined, the difference between the employers and the workers becomes a mere trial of endurance, that is to say, a question of which can afford to hold out the longer. Each day the strike continues the employer sees his hope of profit growing smaller, his machinery getting into worse order, and his loss heavier.

On the other hand, the workers see day after day pass without their receiving any wages, and the Trade Union which has undertaken to support the strikers while they are out of work, sees the money which it has collected in the way of subscriptions from members grow less and less each day.

At such times as these, when the demands

upon the Trades Unions are very heavy, it is the custom to make what is called a "levy" amongst all the members of the Union, for the benefit of those who are out on strike. The levy is a special payment which is demanded from all members of the Union, in order to enable the Council of the Union to obtain a victory in the struggle in which they are engaged.

SUMMARY

STRIKES

1. A strike is a refusal on the part of the workers to continue work until some request which they put forward has been granted.

2. Strikes are resorted to by workers with the object of compelling their employers to do what they would otherwise refuse to do.

3. Strikes are regulated by a law. *A strike for an increase of wages in a falling market* is not likely to succeed.

4. Strikes which seem to be successful are not always profitable to the strikers.

5. On the other hand, strikes which seem to fail may really bring about the object for which they were undertaken.

6. Strikes are best avoided. Argument and reason are better helpers than force.

7. Helping those who are engaged in strikes forms an important part in the work of Trades Unions.

CHAPTER XVI

THE POWER OF PUBLIC OPINION

LIV

A Stronger Power than Strikes

HITHERTO I have been telling you about one method only by which Trades Unions try to improve the position of their members by obtaining for them better wages, or shorter hours, or greater conveniences in their work; but strikes are not the only means by which these ends may be obtained, nor are they the best nor the most powerful means. There is a power which has done more for the good of the workers in this country than all the strikes which were ever begun.

This great helper is the POWER OF PUBLIC OPINION. Nowadays, as you know, almost everything that is said or done in one part of the country is known, by means of the newspapers and by public speeches, in every other part. Whenever any great dispute takes place, whenever any great conflict arises, you are sure to see accounts of it from both parties; and, before very long, people will begin to take sides and to express their opinion as to the rights and wrongs of the dispute.

When so many judges are looking on, and forming an opinion as to the action of those engaged in the dispute, you may be sure that the latter will do all they can, by their actions and by their behaviour, to obtain the goodwill of the public, and not to offend by hasty, unjust, or violent conduct.

Trades Unions and Public Opinion

And so in these important differences which arise from time to time between employers and workers, and in which Trades Unions take so great a part, it becomes every year more important that those who wish to succeed in the struggle should have the good opinion of the public on their side.

Hence it is that both sides in a great strike generally appeal to the public through the newspapers, and each side tries to convince the public that reason and justice are in favour of its claims.

Whenever the public sees a cause conducted with violence, and cruelty, and injustice, it is very sure to condemn it, even though there may be much that is right in the claims which are supported by such bad methods.

In order, therefore, to avoid such condemnation, every effort is made by those who appeal to the public to give no opening for such an unfavourable judgment, and pains are taken to prevent any violent or hasty action on the part of any of those who are concerned in the contest.

And not only is the power of public opinion very

great in restraining violence and encouraging fair dealing and moderation, but it is also a great and direct help towards the attainment of just and reasonable concessions.

Over and over again reforms have been won and concessions made because those who sought them have taken the pains to convince the public that what they required was in itself just, reasonable, and possible.

If we compare the condition of those in this country who worked with their hands fifty years ago, with that of those who do the same work at the present time, we shall find that in a hundred ways the position of the workers is better and happier now than it was then. It is true that there is still much misery and much suffering in the country, but it is beyond doubt that the misery and suffering which we see now was tenfold greater half a century ago.

There have been many causes which helped to bring about this improvement, but the most important changes have certainly been the work of single men or of bodies of men working for the welfare of their countrymen, and winning their way by convincing the public that they were in the right.

LV

Public Opinion and the Corn Laws

Fifty years ago a loaf of bread, which now costs 4d., cost 1s., and the greatest distress was felt throughout the country on account of the scarcity and dearness of food. The chief cause of this scarcity and dearness was the tax that was put upon corn brought into this country from over the sea.

Much more than fifty years ago there were men who were convinced that the tax was wrong and harmful, and should be done away with. But they were few in number, and were powerless to get rid of the Corn Laws by which the duty was imposed. What did these men do? Did they attempt to use violence or encourage others to use it? Millions of men and women were suffering actual hunger on account of the laws, and it would not have been hard to appeal to them to use force to remedy their distress.

But those who were against the Corn Laws did nothing of the kind, they adopted a far better plan. They went throughout the length and breadth of the country explaining to all the world, high and low, rich and poor, the reasons in favour of doing away with the law, and pointing out the benefits which would arise from the free importation of corn.

Victory at Last!

At first they met with great opposition, and everybody seemed against them; but they persevered, and gradually people began to understand their arguments, to see the wisdom of their teaching, and to agree with their advice. At last their reward came, and in the year 1846 the great Act of Parliament, called the Act for the Repeal of the Corn Laws, was passed. Public opinion now supported those whom it had at first condemned, and as soon as public opinion was on the side of the reformers, their opponents were able to resist no longer. So, too, with a number of other reforms.

Public Opinion and Short Hours

Fifty years ago, women and children were employed in our factories for ten, twelve, and fourteen hours a day. Their strength was quite unable to bear such hardship, but as long as any were permitted to work for long hours all were compelled to, for those who refused to work for long hours found that there was no work at all for them to do, and they could not afford to refuse the only terms which were offered to them.

At last, however, a movement arose among a few humane and wise men in favour of shortening the hours of labour for women and children by law. There was great opposition to the change, and much of the opposition came from the very workers whom it was proposed to help. They feared that shorter hours would mean less wages, and their wages were already small enough.

But the friends of the short hours movement stuck to their opinions, and not only did they stick to them, but they reasoned and argued about them with others. They showed that shorter hours meant better health, that better health meant better work, and that better work meant more wages, and not less. And at last, as in the case of the repeal of the Corn Laws, the reformers got public opinion upon their side, and a law was made regulating the employment of women and children, and fixing the number of hours during which they might work.

At present no child under ten is allowed to be employed in a factory at all, and after that age children when employed must not be kept at work for more than half-time. Young persons, by which is meant any worker between fourteen and eighteen years of age, must not work for more than four hours and a half without an interval for rest and refreshment; and no young person or woman can be employed at work in a factory or workshop for more than ten hours a day.

As to the men it is impossible to lay down such strict rules, and to prevent men who are able to take care of themselves from working as long as they please. In practice, however, it has come about that the working hours in most factories have been reduced for men, too, to ten hours, and that work beyond that time is paid for as overtime. This is indeed a happy change from the old times when men, women, and even children, were allowed and compelled to work twelve, fourteen, and even sixteen hours out of the twenty-four.

There can be no doubt that most of the advantages which the friends of short hours hoped for have been obtained, and that the lot of women and children in our factories is far happier and better than it was.

LVI

What the Miners Owe to Public Opinion

Let me give you another instance. There are few occupations more full of danger to those engaged in them than that of coal-mining.

The frequent explosions of gas in the coal-seams are the cause of many terrible accidents to the miners. It is certain that many of these accidents are the result of want of care on the part of those who are charged with the management of the mines, and of proper precautions on the part of those to whom the mines belong. Great efforts have, therefore, been made to compel such persons by law to take every possible care for the preservation of life and limb in the coal-pits, and to secure the punishment of those who neglect to do so.

DOWN IN THE COAL-PIT

By constantly pressing their claims, and by pointing out to the public the dangers which had to be met, those who have interested themselves in this matter have succeeded in obtaining very valuable laws, compelling all those persons to do their duty who were inhumane enough, or careless enough, to neglect it.

One more Victory for Public Opinion

And, lastly, let me give you one more instance of a change which has been brought about in spite of great opposition, by getting public opinion to support the demands of those who sought the change. I give you this example because it concerns a matter in which the Trade Unions have interested themselves very much, and in settling which they have taken a very important part.

Formerly, when a workman met with injury to life or limb while he was working in the service of his employer, he could obtain no compensation for the loss of his time in case of injury, nor could his family obtain compensation for his services in case of his death; and this was true even though the injury was caused by the default or carelessness of his employer.

For instance, if a mason employed in building a house had his leg broken by the fall of a scaffolding pole, and if it appeared that the pole was a rotten one which never ought to have been used at all, still the employer, under the old law, could not be compelled to pay anything towards the support of his workman during the time the latter was out of work.

This plainly was unjust, nor was the injustice removed by saying that the workman ought to have discovered for himself that the pole was rotten, and to have taken good care to keep out of the way of it. It is the duty of an employer to provide good materials, and not to endanger the lives of those who work for him, and it seems strange that this was not always admitted.

A Just Law

The efforts of those who sought to secure justice and protection for the workers have now obtained a still more favourable law than that which I told you of, and at present, not only may a workman who is injured claim compensation from his employer for injuries caused by the fault or neglect of the latter, but he may do so even when the injury is caused by the fault or neglect of an overseer, foreman, or other person conducting the work on behalf of the employer.

It is considered that not only is the employer bound to take all proper care for the safety of those whom he employs, but he is bound to see that the foremen and overseers to whom he entrusts the management of his business are as careful as himself.

If this were not the rule it might often happen that an employer would escape scot-free, whatever accidents took place upon his works, merely because he had chosen to pay people less trustworthy than himself to manage them or to do work in them.

What these Examples Teach

Do not forget what it is I have given you these four examples to prove. They are to prove to you how much good can be done by such bodies as Trades Unions, simply by reason and persuasion, and how important it is that they should get public opinion upon their side whenever they wish to obtain any great advantage.

SUMMARY

HOW CHANGES SHOULD BE BROUGHT ABOUT

1. The power of public opinion is greater than that of the strongest Trades Union.

2. It is the power of public opinion which has brought about most of the great changes which have helped the workers in this country.

3. Those who desire to effect great changes should therefore try to win public opinion to their side.

4. Reason and persuasion are better instruments than force and fear.

CHAPTER XVII

THE EVIL FRUIT OF LAW-BREAKING

LVII

Some Dangers of Trades Unions

I HAVE spoken in the last two or three chapters of the good that may be done by Trades Unions acting wisely and justly. Every year the Unions learn more clearly how much can be done by moderation and reason, and how little can be accomplished by violence and injustice.

The account that I have given you would not, however, be complete if I were to make no mention of those occasions on which Trades Unions have allowed themselves to be carried away by evil counsels, and have tried to obtain their objects by violence, cruelty, and injustice.

How Harm is Done to a Good Cause

It is certain that much harm has been done to the cause of the workers, and many wise reforms which they have now obtained have been hindered and put off, by the unwise action of a few Trades Unions; it is therefore well to know what kind of mistakes have been made, in order that they may be avoided in the future.

The Use of Force

There are several ways in which a Trades Union may use force and violence with the hope of compelling others to assent to its demands. It may use violence against its own members, and may compel them to take part in, or refrain from taking part in, some action against their will; it may try to terrify and injure workmen belonging to the same trade, but not members of the Union; it may use force or threats against those who give employment; it may try to frighten those appointed to carry out the law, and to prevent them doing their duty; and, lastly, it may endeavour, by creating alarm and by encouraging riots, to frighten people who have nothing to do with the trade, into giving their support to the cause of the Union.

Whenever a Trades Union, or indeed any other body, tries to obtain its objects in any of the ways mentioned above, there can be only one judgment upon its action. It is bad, and utterly to be condemned.

Who have a Right to Use Force

To begin with, nobody has a right to use force against his neighbours except those who are especially appointed by the law to do so, and who receive their authority from the whole country, according to the law of the land. Therefore, any attempt by other persons to use force is an offence against the law.

Moreover, any attempt to compel people to do what they do not wish to do, or to prevent them doing what they wish to do, and have a right to do, is an interference with that freedom which we in this country are so proud of, and which we have only won after so many struggles.

The Mistakes of Trades Unions

Occasionally members of Trades Unions have forgotten or neglected these truths, and have tried to prevent others enjoying that liberty which they would be the first to claim for themselves.

Sometimes, as I told you, they have used violence, or the threat of violence, against members of the Union, in order to make them assist in some particular action. More often it has happened that the threats and violence have been directed against others in the same trade, who have refused to act with the members of the Trades Union. This is what has frequently happened in the case of strikes, and it is easy to see how the evil arises, and how it is that men are tempted into such bad courses.

From what I said about strikes in the last chapter you will understand that, in order that a strike may be successful, the employer of the men upon strike must be unable to replace the strikers by other workmen, or must be, at any rate, unable to do so without great loss and difficulty. But in many trades the number of workers is very great, and some of them are not members of any Union at all, and it is therefore often easy for the employer to replace his workers by men who do not belong to a Union.

LVIII

The History of a Bad Strike

This is an account of what happened not long ago in such a trade:—The members of a Trades Union, working in one place, determined to strike for an increase of wages, and accordingly they all stopped work, and left the employer to do his best without them. The employer, however, refused to grant the increase, believing that he could get the work done at the old rate by other workers. Accordingly he gave notice that work was to be had by all who chose to take it at the wages he offered.

Now, there were many workers in the trade who were not members of the Union, and among them were some who were not only willing but very glad to take the work at the wages offered. They had bound themselves by no rule to obey the orders of the Trades Union, and accordingly they came to the employer and offered their services.

When the members of the Trades Union saw this they were much alarmed, for it was plain that if the new men were taken on, not only would the strike fail, but they themselves, instead of getting higher wages, would get no wages at all. They determined, therefore, that the new workers should not be allowed to undertake the work, and they decided to prevent them by the worst possible means.

The tools of the new-comers were broken or taken away, the men themselves were followed from place to place, and threatened with violence if they did not either go away or agree to support the claims of the Union; and at last, from threats, the members of the Trades Union proceeded to actual violence, and some of the new workers were attacked and injured.

I have told you this story because it is an example of what has happened on many occasions when Trades Unions have followed evil counsels, and have tried to obtain their ends by injustice and cruelty.

Fortunately, such things are less common now than they were, for the leaders of the Trades Unions have learnt to put no confidence in such bad methods, and have learnt too that the cause which they have at heart—that of bettering the condition of their fellow-workmen—is injured in the eyes of the public, who are sure to condemn the use of violence.

LIX

Violence Always Wrong

Many excuses have been made at different times for those who have tried to win an advantage by interfering with others. It has been said that those who take advantage of their fellow-workmen at a time when they are fighting for better wages and better hours, are traitors to the cause, and are fairly made the objects of hatred and persecution by those whom they interfere with. But this is a very bad and false excuse.

If a man break the law, and the offence can be proved against him, the law will punish him. If he has not broken the law, the law will not punish him, and no one has any right to step in and say, "This man has not broken the law of the land, but he has broken the law of my Society or my Union, and I and my comrades will punish him for doing so."

If once men were allowed to take the law into their own hands, and to decide whether or not others were to be punished, there would soon be an end to all law, and we should find ourselves back in the old barbarous times, when might was right, and brute force stood in the place of justice.

The Old Way and the New

It is well for us to understand clearly how true this is. We have only got to look back into history to see what happened when "might was right," when the only law was the law of the strongest, and when each man was a judge in his own cause. In those times it was always "the weakest who went to the wall," the poor and the defenceless who suffered. On the following page you have a picture of the way in which quarrels used to be settled at one time in this country. A great noble who had quarrelled with his neighbour, instead of bringing his case before a court of justice and getting a decision as to his right, took the law in his own hands, called his friends together, and went up to his neighbour's castle and challenged him, as is represented in the picture, to settle their dispute by fighting about it. And you may be sure that while the strong settled their differences by fighting, the differences between those who were strong and those who were weak were simply settled by the ruin and injury of the latter.

And so if we go back still further into history, or

THE OLD WAY: THE CHALLENGE

look at countries in our own day where there is no regular law, we shall see fierce struggles between savage men, cruel murders, and acts of private revenge. It is back to such a state of things that we are beginning to go directly we allow anybody in our country to take the law into his own hands.

Next is a picture of what we have put in the place of the challenge and the battle of the old days. The picture shows you a "writ," which is the summons sent from the courts of justice in the name of the Queen, calling upon the person named in it to submit the matter of

THE NEW WAY: A WRIT
OF THE HIGH COURT OF JUSTICE

difference between him and his neighbour to be decided upon by a judge according to law.

You will see that Mr. Smith makes a claim upon Mr. Brown, and instead of threatening Mr. Brown with violence, or attacking his house, and injuring his property, he goes to the courts of justice, and at his request a writ is sent to Mr. Brown ordering him to come up and answer to Mr. Smith's claim. If Mr. Brown makes no answer, then the law will suppose he has no answer to make, and decision will be given in favour of Mr. Smith (who is called the plaintiff, or person making the complaint). If Mr. Brown (the defendant) says that he has an answer to Mr. Smith's claim, then the judge will hear what he has to say, and if he thinks he is right, he will decide in his favour; if, on the other hand, he thinks the plaintiff is right, then the judge will decide for him, and Mr. Brown will have to pay what is claimed from him. In this way all is done peaceably and in order, and this is the only plan which ought ever to be allowed in any country.

The Line between Right and Wrong

And the same thing is true of agreements made between members of Trades Unions. All the members of a Trades Union agree together to observe certain rules as long as they are members of the Union; and if these rules are just and legal in themselves, the law allows the Union to insist upon their being observed.

For instance, it is often the rule that a member of the Union may be fined if he breaks the rules which he has agreed to keep, and that the money which he has paid to the Union may be taken for that purpose.

Or it may be the rule that in certain cases he may be turned out of the Union altogether, and the money which he has paid may be kept and never returned to him. The law allows this to be done. Nor has the member who is turned out any right to complain, for he knew what he was about when he agreed to obey the rules, and he has himself chosen to break them.

But the Trades Union has no right whatever to go one inch outside the agreement which it has made with its members. Nor has it any right to make them fulfil their agreement in any other way than that which the law of the land allows.

And if a Trades Union has no right to compel its own members—who have of their own accord agreed to observe its rules—to do what they do not wish to do, or to refrain from doing what they want to do, still less has it any right to compel those who are not members to obey its wishes. In whatever way it be made, such an attempt is contrary to law and to justice, and ought to be condemned and, if possible, punished.

Interference with the Lawful Rights of Others

And when I speak of violence and threats, and condemn the use of them, I do not mean only such violence as consists in doing bodily injury to those whom it is intended to frighten; nor, when I speak of threats, do I mean only such threats as are openly spoken and written.

Many ways of interfering with the liberty and happiness of men have been discovered which do not always end either in open violence or open threats. Sometimes, indeed, this interference is practised in such a way that those who try to benefit by it persuade themselves that it is a just and blameless way of helping their cause.

Exclusive Dealing

Such, for instance, is the practice of what is called "exclusive dealing," which may be made into one of the most terrible forms of persecution and cruelty. This practice of exclusive dealing has many forms and many names, but in its chief points it remains the same under all its forms. Those who decide to adopt the plan agree together, in the first place, only to buy from and sell to—in other words, only to deal with—those whom they consider their friends.

But the real object of such an agreement is generally not to confer a benefit upon friends, but to inflict an injury upon an enemy. The agreement to deal with one man generally means an agreement *not* to deal with another; in other words, it is an attempt to make another man alter his opinion or alter his actions by inflicting suffering and loss upon him.

LX

From Bad to Worse

Even to do this much is, as I shall explain to you, wrong and unjust. But, unfortunately, it very seldom happens that those who adopt these methods stop at this point, or are contented even with the suffering which they inflict in this way. It almost always happens that those who begin to use force under any shape for the attainment of their objects, are not content with such a method as this.

In order to terrify or distress a man, it is not only necessary that those who have a quarrel with him should refuse to deal with him, should shun him, and refuse to have anything to do with him; it is necessary that others, who have no quarrel with him, should likewise be compelled to avoid him.

Then, many who have nothing to do with the dispute are brought into it, and are compelled to assist in making their neighbour unhappy and poor. If any one of these persons refuses to join in the agreement, then he too must be made to feel the displeasure of those about him by the same sort of persecution.

And lastly, it is almost certain to happen in a country where men are accustomed to liberty and are proud of it, that some will be found to resist persuasions and threats, and such men will resist to the last, and will refuse to pay any attention to the requests made to them.

If such be the case, there is only one way in which these men can be made to submit and prevented from spoiling the whole plan, and that is by the use of actual violence. And so, in fact, it has been over and over again where men have tried to compel those who differ from them to change their minds by the threat of "exclusive dealing," that what has begun in a simple agreement between friends, has ended in deeds of blood and violence.

I told you that even an agreement not to have any dealings with a man in order to compel him to do what he does not wish to do, or to prevent him doing what he has a right to do, was to be condemned, even though no actual violence were used. And so it is, as you will see for yourselves in a moment if you consider the matter.

It is certain that those who agree together for such a purpose hope to compel another to do that which he would not do of his own free will. It is plain that it is not by argument or reason that they expect to move him, for then there would be no need for them to combine at all.

What they really hope to do, is to make the man against whom they direct their "exclusive dealing" suffer for not acting as they wish. They may inflict this suffering in many ways: by injuring his trade, by damaging his credit or his good name, by rendering his life uncomfortable, by causing him to be hated or despised by others; but in each case their object is to make him suffer, and to induce him to escape from his suffering by agreeing with those who have combined against him.

Fine Names do not Make Good Actions

Now, it is possible to call such a plan as this by a great many fine names, and to make many excuses for it, but in the end the fact remains, that here are a number of people trying to punish a man for acting in accordance with the law.

They are either injuring a man, or threatening him with injury, because he does not choose to obey them. There can be no doubt about this, for unless a man were either injured or afraid of being injured, he would certainly not do what he did not wish to do, or refrain from doing what he wished to do and had a right to do.

The Law Alone may Punish

But, as I have told you more than once in this book, it is the law alone which has the right to punish, and then only when those whom it punishes are proved to have broken the law.

Nor is this all. So careful is the law not to punish unjustly, that every man, rich or poor, receives a fair hearing and a patient trial before he is condemned; and when he is condemned his punishment is not fixed according to the will of the judge, but is awarded in accordance with the law, which lays down the exact penalty for each offence. In such a way only can justice be done and cruelty and injustice be avoided.

Illegal, Unjust, Cruel

Those who join together to compel a man to act with them in the way I have described, forget all these truths.

In the first place, *they take the law into their own hands;* in the second place, *they punish a man, not for breaking the law, but for acting in accordance with it;* in the third place, *they are judges in their own cause,* for it is almost always with a view of getting some advantage for themselves that men combine in this way; fourthly—and this is most important to remember—*the punishment is not in proportion to the offence;* and lastly, *the person who brings the charge is not examined as to its truth, and the person against whom it is brought has no opportunity of speaking for himself.* In every point the laws of justice and truth are forgotten and abandoned.

When once this kind of persecution has begun there is no foretelling where it will stop; and so far from its falling equally upon all who are condemned, it is always the weak, the friendless, the unfortunate who suffer most from it.

LXI

The Lesson to be Learnt

Therefore you will see that it is never just or right for a Trades Union, or any other body of men, to try and obtain what they want by causing pain, suffering, or loss to others. Even if those who are opposed to them are really acting wrongly or hardly, it is still wrong for anyone not specially appointed by the law to try and punish them, for that would be breaking the law in order to maintain it.

I have told you about some of the ways in which Trades Unions have from time to time sought to gain their objects by bad methods. Whether it be by threats and violence offered to members of the Union, or by threats and violence used against those who are not members; whether it be by attempts to frighten the public or to frighten the officers of the law that the Union tries to compel others to do what they do not wish to do, or to prevent them doing what they have a right to do, the result is the same.

Cruelty, injustice, and force are put in the place of honesty, justice, and law, and harm is done to those who are guilty of these actions, and to the country which suffers from their commission.

Happily, these things are so clear that they have long been understood by the members of the Trades Unions, and year by year they have learnt to avoid such methods of helping or trying to help their cause.

The more clearly the injustice of such methods is seen, the more easy it will be to avoid being led into adopting them; and therefore it is useful, while speaking of Trades Unions and the good that they do, to recall also some of the dangers to which they have at times been exposed, and from which even now they sometimes suffer.

SUMMARY

THE EVIL FRUIT OF LAW-BREAKING

1. Trades Unions have sometimes tried to gain their ends by bad means.

2. It is necessary to learn about their mistakes in order to avoid them in the future.

3. The use of violence by those who are acting for themselves, and not on behalf of the law, is always wrong.

4. It is as bad to threaten violence as to use it.

5. The Legislature alone has the right to punish.

6. There is only one way of making or altering the law in this country, and that is by an Act of Parliament. Anyone who tries to alter the law by other means breaks the law, and deserves severe punishment.

Part IV

WORK AND WORKERS

"IT IS ONLY BY LABOUR THAT THOUGHT CAN BE MADE HEALTHY, AND ONLY BY THOUGHT THAT LABOUR CAN BE MADE HAPPY; AND THE TWO CANNOT BE SEPARATED WITH IMPUNITY."

Ruskin.

CHAPTER XVIII

WORK AND WORKERS

LXII

Who are the Workers?

In the previous chapters of this book you have read a great deal about work and workers; and as all of you will, I hope, become workers and hard workers some day, I shall say something in this last chapter which may encourage and help you in the work you will each have to undertake, if your lives are to be of any use to yourselves or to other people.

Working to Live

Nearly every man has to work for his living. Many women and children have to do the same to earn their bread, and since work must form so great a part of the lives of all of us, it is worth while to consider carefully some of the most important questions connected with work and workers.

Living to Work

I said that nearly every man was compelled to work for his living. There are persons, however, as you all

227

know, who are rich enough to be able to live without having to earn money at all. There are several ways in which men may become rich and independent of daily work.

They may be owners of property which has been left to them by their ancestors or relations; they may have saved enough, or earned enough, during their lives to be able to stop working, and to live on what they have earned; or they may be the owners of property which has become very valuable all of a sudden; for instance, they may own land on which a coal-mine is discovered; or, lastly, they may have made some discovery, or invention, which turns out to be very valuable, and brings them a large sum of money.

In all these ways men may become so rich that they do not need to work for their living. But it does not follow that because a man does not work for his living he does not work at all. On the contrary, it very often happens that those who are free to be idle if they please are to be found amongst the hardest workers.

There are many ways in which such men can and do occupy their time. They may devote it to the service of their country as great statesmen do, or they may devote it directly to helping and relieving those who are in distress and poverty.

Such was the work of Mrs. Fry at the beginning of this century. The greater number of the gaols in this country were shamefully conducted, the prisoners were ill-treated, the food was bad, and, worse than all, no sort of distinction was made between the different classes

MRS. FRY VISITING THE GAOLS

of prisoners, and every one who was sent to gaol was thrown into the company of the very worst and most degraded criminals.

Thus many who might have been warned by their first punishment, and have taken to honest lives, were led away during their imprisonment by the vile companions whom they found there, and came out at the end of their time far worse than when they went in. You can well believe that these overcrowded gaols, full of violent and bad men and women, ill-managed, close, and filthy, were no pleasant places for a delicate woman to enter.

Nevertheless, Mrs. Fry devoted herself to the cause of those who were in prison, and never wearied of going from gaol to gaol, helping those who were willing to accept her help, calling attention to the mismanagement and cruelty that went on, and persuading those whose business it was to look after the prisons to do their work with greater thought and humanity. This country owes much to the efforts of Mrs. Fry and those who worked with her; and the work she did, though she earned no money by it, was of the highest and best kind which any man or woman can undertake.

Such work also was that of Lord Shaftesbury, who gave up the whole of a long life to the cause of helping others, and lessening the suffering and misery of his poorer fellow-countrymen.

LXIII

Leisure Well Occupied

Men may prefer to continue working at their own business, and to go on making money, although there is really no need for them to do so, or they may occupy themselves in studying some great branch of learning, or in practising some art, whereby the knowledge of men is increased, and their opportunities of enjoyment enlarged.

In all these ways, and in many others, those who are not compelled to work for their living may still work as hard as those who depend upon their work for their daily bread; and all time that is honourably spent in this way is well and usefully spent.

Of course, on the other hand, there are often cases when men use their riches only for their own amusement, and their own self-indulgence, and such a use must always be bad and harmful. But what I want you to understand is that it is not the mere making and earning of money that is so important, but rather the way in which a man's time is spent, whether he be earning money to spend, or spending money that he already possesses.

The Value of Work

It is said sometimes by people who have not given much thought to what they are saying, that work is a very noble and good thing in itself, and that the more work people do the better it is for them. But if you think for a moment you will see how easily great mistakes may be made by those who talk of work in this way.

In the 17th century there lived in France a clever and beautiful woman named the Marchioness of Brinvilliers. She was rich and proud, and had many friends, and a good position in the world. But though she was rich enough to live a life of ease and comfort without working at all, she nevertheless spent many hours in close study and hard work. And what was the work she did?

Shut up in a secret chamber, she worked, with the help of her lover, and of a clever but bad man named Exili, to find out the most deadly forms of poison by which the lives of men could be taken away.

THE MARCHIONESS AT WORK

232

She worked hard to discover these terrible secrets, and to acquire this dangerous knowledge; and when she had found some draught or some powder which she could give without risk of being found out, she used to contrive that it should be placed in the food or the drink of those whom she hated or feared, and so made them the victims of her cruel and wicked arts.

You will not require to be told that the work of the Marchioness Brinvilliers was neither noble nor good, and that the harder she worked the more certainly must she have become cruel, hard-hearted, and hateful. Plainly, such work would have been better left undone.

Good Work

But now turn from the secret chamber of the Marchioness to the study of the great doctor, Sir James Simpson. He, too, is working hard with brain and hand; he, too, is working with poisons so deadly that a few drops of the clear mixture in his hand will send a fellow-creature into a sleep so deep that it ends only in death.

But what is the end for which he is working, and what is the puzzle which he is trying to solve? The liquid in his hand is chloroform, and the puzzle he is trying to solve is how the power of this terrible poison can be best utilised to diminish pain and suffering in the world, and to make the lives of men and women happier.

And Sir James Simpson and others who have worked with him have found out the answer to the problem, and have discovered and perfected the use of chloroform, so that doctors all over the world can make use of its wonderful power for the good of those who are in pain.

The Use of Chloroform

Perhaps some of you may not know what this chloroform is that I am speaking of, and, indeed, I trust none of you may ever need its help. But though you may never yourselves require it, it is well that you should know what is its nature and use. Chloroform, which Sir James Simpson and others have taught us to use, is a liquid which, when exposed to the air, rapidly changes into vapour, and so powerful are the effects of this vapour over the human body that anyone who breathes it loses for a time all sense of pain, and, indeed, all feeling whatever.

SIR JAMES SIMPSON
Born, 1811; *died* 1870.

It is this power of taking away pain that doctors have made use of; and when they are compelled to perform some painful operation upon a sick or injured person—to cut off a leg or an arm, to cut or to pierce some tender part of the body—they first make the patient breathe in a deep draught of the vapour of chloroform. Very soon, under the power of the chloroform, all sense of feeling leaves the patient, and while he lies thus unconscious and unmoved the surgeon performs the necessary operation.

Then, when the sense of feeling returns, the patient

wakes up to find that all is over, and that, thanks to the wonderful discovery, he has been spared the agony which he would undoubtedly have suffered if the surgeon had done his work without the aid of chloroform.

I have told you the story of the Marchioness of Brinvilliers, and I have given you a short account of the discovery and use of chloroform, to show you that work in itself and by itself is neither good nor bad, but that its badness or its goodness will depend upon the spirit in which it is done, and the object for which it is undertaken. The Marchioness worked hard, and worked with great cleverness and skill, but her work was directed to the worst ends, the infliction of pain and suffering upon innocent people. Such work was bad and hateful.

The great doctor, too, worked hard and skilfully, and the materials with which he worked were much the same as those used by the great poisoner, but every hour that he spent in his experiments was devoted to serving the cause of his fellow-creatures, and in seeking to diminish the suffering of human beings. His work was truly noble.

LXIV

The Nature of Work

Then, again, it is not uncommon to hear people talk of certain kinds of work as "degrading," and say that it is certain to lower and injure the character of those who do it.

It is quite true that there are some kinds of work which are really of this nature. For instance, no man can go on working long at an occupation which involves trickery and deceit, or which can only succeed by inflicting pain or loss upon other people, without becoming the worse for what he does.

Degrading Work

For example, there are some manufacturers in this country who have been accustomed to make cloth or cotton stuffs for sale among the Chinese and other Eastern people, and who have not been ashamed to add clay, and other substances, to the articles they made in order to make them weigh heavily, and to lead the buyers to believe that they were obtaining good cloth or cotton for their money, instead of stuff covered with clay, which would wear off as soon as the material was washed.

It would be impossible for a man who made money by practising this deceit to carry on such work without being the worse for it. Such work is in itself "degrading," for it cannot be done without perpetual dishonesty.

In the same way, a man who makes his living by writing bad and harmful books does work which is degrading, for a man cannot use his powers to lower and injure other people without injuring and lowering himself.

In this sense, therefore, it is true that there are some kinds of work which are in themselves shameful and degrading. But we ought always to be very careful how we use such expressions of the work men are compelled to do for their living.

Dull Work

It is said sometimes that certain kinds of work which are very disagreeable, or which are very dull and stupid, and require neither skill nor knowledge to perform, are degrading. This is not true. No honest work is in itself degrading, or can become so. On the contrary, every man who works hard and well at an honourable occupation in order to earn his daily bread, is doing what is both wise and right.

It is true that there are some occupations which we should be very glad to see done away with, not because they are degrading, but because they prevent a man or woman who is engaged in them from improving any of the great powers of mind and body which have been given to all of us.

"Human" Machines

In a great steel pen manufactory, for instance, every pen has to pass through many hands before it is finished and ready to be used. The steel must be made and rolled and smoothed, the pen must be cut from the steel, and shaped and pointed and stamped and polished; and each of these things is done separately by a different machine.

Now, each such machine must be looked after by a separate person, who has nothing to do all the time he or she is at work but to put pens into one side of the machine and take them out at the other. In fact, the person who looks after the machine becomes, for the time, only a part, and not a very important part, of the machine itself.

Their Effect

You can easily fancy that if such a worker were to go on working during the whole of his waking hours instead of eight or nine hours only, before long he would become as senseless as the machine which he looked after. Nothing that such a man did would help him to exercise either his mind or his body.

Every man and woman is born with the power of loving and hoping, of thinking and acting, of learning and using knowledge. But a man who puts pens into one side of a machine and takes them out at the other is not taught by the work he does to do any of these things which Nature has fitted him to do, and intends him to do.

Of course, I do not mean that those who are engaged in such work as this, those who do the work of machines only, are without love or hope, without the power of thinking and acting, of learning and using their knowledge. On the contrary, many thousands of those who are thus engaged have learnt to make the best possible use of the gifts which Nature has given them.

But what I want you to understand is that it is not from their work that they learn to improve their minds or their bodies. If they did not learn elsewhere the work itself would teach them nothing, and though not in itself degrading, it would in the end be sure to make the workers no better than the machines which they look after.

Therefore it is most important that too great a part of a man's life should not be given up to work which helps to make a machine of him, for it is only during the time that he is not so employed that he is able to improve all those qualities which make him a good man and a good citizen.

For these reasons we ought always to wish that men and women should not be engaged for very long at a time upon work which is only the work of a machine, and which in itself does nothing to make them wiser, happier, stronger, or better.

It is the duty of every man to get his own living and to support those who depend on him; and if in order to do this he has to do work of the kind I have described he is honourably and well employed, because he is doing his duty. But, as to the work itself, it cannot be called either good or bad, honourable or dishonourable. The spirit in which it is done may be very honourable, but of the work it can only be said that it is merely a means of earning wages, and teaches nothing to those who do it.

LXV

The Best Kind of Work

There are, however, many occupations which are very different from those I have described. There are many kinds of work which in themselves help to educate and strengthen the mind or the body of those who undertake them.

All work which requires skill, forethought, or judgment is in itself a help and an education to the worker. There are, of course, many degrees of such work—some teaching much, some little. A ploughman can drive a furrow well or ill; his skill consists in driving it straight and even, and each day that he works he can be improving in his art and learning to do better one day than he did the day before.

Hand Work

A joiner need never come to an end of his art. He may begin as an apprentice by learning to square a rough piece of wood, or to hammer a nail straight into a board, and, by using his brains and practising his hands, he may become the maker or designer of the most beautiful and costly furniture, such as that which is now bought for thousands of pounds, and specimens of which you may see in many museums.

Head Work

And what is true of a man who works with his hands is true of a man who works with his head only. A doctor begins when he is still a young student to learn the lessons of his profession. He goes into the hospitals and examines the different cases of illness and accident which he finds there. He also receives instruction in making up medicine, and learns what are the proper drugs to use, and in what quantities they should be mixed.

When the medical student has been five or six years learning from what he sees and what he reads, if his knowledge be sufficient, he is allowed to make use of it and to start in the world as a doctor or surgeon.

Living and Learning

But do not suppose for a moment that, because he has now been allowed to get to work in his profession, he has ceased to be a learner. Quite the contrary. No day passes in which a doctor or a surgeon does not

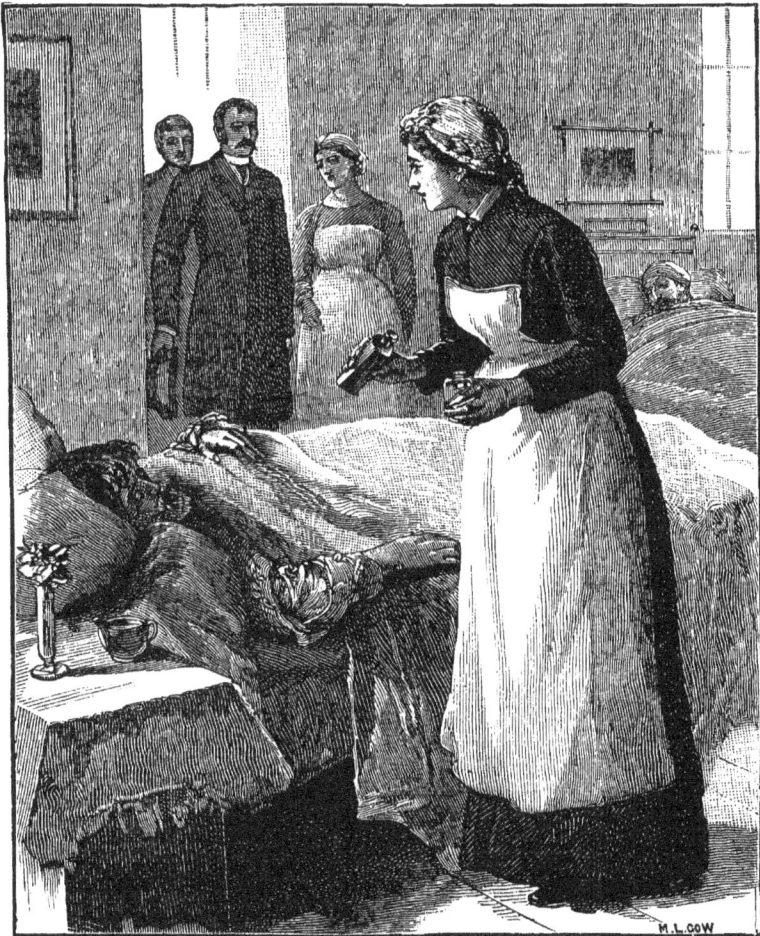

NURSE AND DOCTOR: TWO NOBLE PROFESSIONS

learn something more of his art—the nature of some sickness, the course of some fever, or the best way of curing some particular disorder.

In the profession of a doctor there is no end to the knowledge which may be acquired, and the work which is done not only exercises and improves the mind, but is in itself a noble and splendid occupation, the object of which is to diminish suffering and pain among men.

Brain Work and Heart Work

The man of letters, too—the man, I mean, whose work it is to write books, poetry, history, biography, books on science, or whatever they may be—finds in his work a daily opportunity of using the best powers

ROBERT BURNS

which have been given to him. The poet exercises his imagination, and tells of love and hope, of sorrow and gladness, of courage and fear. There is nothing great and lovable and worthy in all the world which a poet cannot study and sing of in his poems.

The historian studies the past, and tries to bring before our minds the truth about the lives and fortunes of those who have gone before us in our own country and in other lands. He must be accurate and truthful, careful in finding out the real facts which he wishes to tell the world, and clear in his way of writing them down, so that they may be rightly understood.

The Lessons of Work

Nor is it only those trades and professions of which I have spoken that are in themselves useful and helpful to those who know how to follow them wisely. Luckily there are many hundreds of occupations which, in a greater or lesser degree, help to train and improve the mind and the body.

The labourer in the fields not only may learn to do his hedging and ditching, his ploughing and reaping, better from day to day, but living as he does so much in the open air, and seeing all the wonderful changes of Nature, he may learn to understand and to admire what he sees.

It was while following the plough that Robert Burns, the great poet of Scotland, stored his mind with many of the beautiful thoughts which his poems contain. It was while following the plough that he crushed a little mountain daisy with the share. His poet's mind pitied the poor flower, and he has left us the beautiful "Verses to a Mountain Daisy," which tell us his thoughts—

The Poet Ploughman

"Wee, modest, crimson-tippèd flower,
  Thou's met me in an evil hour;
For I maun[19] crush amang the stoure[20]
      Thy slender stem:
To spare thee now is past my power,
      Thou bonny gem.

"Alas! it's no thy neibor sweet,
  The bonny lark, companion meet,
Bending thee 'mang[21] the dewy weet,[22]
      Wi' speckled breast,
When upward springing, blithe, to greet
      The purpling east.

"Cauld blew the bitter-biting north
  Upon thy early, humble birth;
Yet cheerfully thou glinted[23] forth
      Amid the storm:
Scarce reared above the parent earth
      Thy tender form.

"The flaunting flowers our gardens yield,
  High sheltering woods and wa's[24] maun shield,
But thou, beneath the random bield[25]
      O' clod or stane,

[19]Maun = must
[20]Stoure = dust
[21]Mang = among
[22]Weet = wheat
[23]Glinted = peeped
[24]Wa's = walls
[25]Random bield = accidental shelter

244

Adorns the histie stibble[26] field
Unseen alane.

"There, in thy scanty mantle clad,
Thy snawie bosom sunward spread,
Thou lifts thy unassuming head
In humble guise:
But now the *share* uptears thy bed,
And low thou lies!'

*   *   *   *   *

LXVI

The Soldier, the Weaver, the Seamstress

As a ploughman, if he uses his eyes and his mind, may learn, not only to be a good ploughman, but something more, so may a soldier learn, not only how to shoulder a gun and to march in rank, but to be faithful, brave, watchful, obedient, and ready to sacrifice himself for others.

A weaver may learn, not only to finish a piece of cloth or stuff cleverly and neatly, but may also become acquainted with the art of designing patterns, of judging what colour or what mixture of colours gives the best appearance, or is most likely to suit the taste of those who buy. A weaver who can do this has occupation for the eye and the brain as well as for the hand.

A woman who works with her needle need never come to an end of the new uses to which it may be put,

---

[26]Histie stibble = barren stubble

and while, on the one hand, she is learning to be neat, quick, and handy, she may be practising many other qualities besides. In cutting out clothes for herself and her children she may exercise her skill and good taste; in mending and darning she may show her ingenuity and her love of economy; in doing dull work well and honestly she may give proof of her patience; and in teaching others what she knows, she will have plenty of opportunities of helping others to share the knowledge she has acquired.

I have told you about all these different kinds of work, and the opportunities they afford to the workers to become better and wiser, in order to make you understand the real lesson which I want to teach you in this chapter.

If you have followed me you will have learnt what I mean in the following sentence:—

All work which is honestly done, and which is not done for a bad purpose, is good, but it is not all equally good.

What to Work for

Men and women have to work in this world in order to earn enough to buy food and drink, clothes and lodging for themselves and their families. In other words, they work to live.

But what do they live for? They live to make the best and noblest use of the gifts which they possess. They have hearts to love, brains to think and contrive, hands and feet to carry out the will of their heart and brain; they have bodies which feel pain, and minds which suffer sometimes more than their bodies, and thus they know what suffering is in others, and how good a thing it is to help those who are in want, distress, or pain.

It is to use all these great and wonderful gifts in the best way and to the greatest extent that men and women live, or ought to live; and therefore it is that that work which best helps a man or woman to live their life in the best way is really the best work.

Golden Rules

No one can form general rules, or say this work or that work is the best. Some are fitted for one kind, some for another. But you may depend upon it that though there is no general rule which can be written down in a book, there is none the less a rule which every man, woman, and child can find out for his or her own particular case.

Whether it be doing lessons or governing the country, whether it be making bricks or painting pictures, there is always an answer to the question, "Is this work helping me to live well?" which the worker, whether he be scholar or Prime Minister, bricklayer or artist, can put for himself if he only choose to, and to which he can get a true answer if he pleases.

SUMMARY

WORK AND WORKERS

1. Everybody ought to be occupied, but it is not necessary that everybody should work for his living.

2. Leisure well occupied may be made a blessing to mankind.

3. Work is not in itself good or bad. It is good or bad according to the object with which it is undertaken, and the spirit in which it is performed.

4. Some work is truly degrading. Some work does neither good nor harm to the worker, is neither degrading nor helpful. Some work is in itself noble and helpful. There should be none of the first, as little as may be of the second, and as much as possible of the third kind.

www.ingramcontent.com/pod-product-compliance
Lightning Source LLC
Chambersburg PA
CBHW021048090426
42738CB00006B/245